SpringerBriefs in Computer Science

Series Editors

Stan Zdonik
Peng Ning
Shashi Shekhar
Jonathan Katz
Xindong Wu
Lakhmi C. Jain
David Padua
Xuemin Shen
Borko Furht
V. S. Subrahmanian

T0211621

For further volumes:
http://www.springer.com/series/10028

Silvio Cesare · Yang Xiang

Software Similarity
and Classification

Silvio Cesare
School of Information Technology
Deakin University
221 Burwood Highway
Burwood
VIC 3125
Australia

Yang Xiang
School of Information Technology
Deakin University
221 Burwood Highway
Burwood
VIC 3125
Australia

ISSN 2191-5768
ISBN 978-1-4471-2908-0
DOI 10.1007/978-1-4471-2909-7
Springer London Heidelberg New York Dordrecht

e-ISSN 2191-5776
e-ISBN 978-1-4471-2909-7

British Library Cataloguing in Publication Data
A catalogue record for this book is available from the British Library

Library of Congress Control Number: 2012933433

Printed on acid free paper

Springer is part of Springer Science+Business Media (www.springer.com)

Preface

This book is a unique analysis of four seemingly disparate fields of study. Those fields are malware classification, software theft detection, plagiarism detection and code clone detection. These areas of study are all closely intertwined and share much of the same underlying theory. However, this was not always apparent to us. Before writing this book, our research goals were in malware classification. However, this grew outwards as we began to see that those other fields of study gave an applicable theory and analysis techniques that could be useful in our own work. The final result is a merging of these fields and a demonstration that a unified theory can be created and shared equally between them.

The target audiences of this book are researchers looking at performing new investigation who are seeking a summary of the discipline and software engineers who are looking to implement a solution for their own particular application. Researchers will benefit from understanding the base theory that enables new techniques to be critically analysed. Software engineers will benefit from selecting the appropriate components from the whole theory and applying them in their own software.

We hope that the reader will enjoy this book and see it as filling a gap which currently exists in constructing a theory to describe the problems in software similarity and classification.

Acknowledgments

We would like to acknowledge with gratitude some support from research grants that we have received, in particular, Australian Research Council (ARC) Discovery Project DP1095498, ARC Linkage Project LP100100208, Deakin University Central Research Grant Scheme (CRGS) Projects RM22414 and RM24147. Although the research grants were not directly used to support the writing of the book, some interesting research results presented in the book were from our papers which are partially supported through these grants.

We would like to thank Prof. Wanlei Zhou, the Head of School of Information Technology, Deakin University, for his encouragement and support of the research environment, where we spent productive time working on this book.

We are grateful to the family of each of ours for their consistent and persistent love and support. Silvio would like to present the book to Maxine and Paloma. Yang would like to present the book to Abby, David, Julia, and Ella.

December 2011   Silvio and Yang

Contents

Chapter 1
Introduction

Abstract This chapter introduces the major applications related to software similarity and classification. The applications include malware classification, software theft detection, plagiarism detection and code clone detection. The motivations for these applications are examined and an underlying theory is formalized. This theory is based on extracting signatures from programs, known as birthmarks, that are amenable to approximate matching that tells us how similar those programs are.

Keywords Software similarity · Software classification · Malware classification · Software theft detection · Plagiarism detection · Code clone detection

1.1 Background

The software similarity problem is to determine the similarity between two pieces of software. Software that is similar has a common origin. This allows for relationships between software to be inferred such as when used in evolutionary trees to identify a software's ancestry and derivatives. The software classification problem is to assign classes to software. For example, software may be labelled as belonging to the class of malicious programs, or the class of non malicious programs. Software similarity and software classification are closely related and based on the problem of feature extraction. Feature extraction concerns itself with identifying invariant properties of a program.

S. Cesare and Y. Xiang, *Software Similarity and Classification*,
SpringerBriefs in Computer Science, DOI: 10.1007/978-1-4471-2909-7_1,
© The Author(s) 2012

1.2 Applications of Software Similarity and Classification

A number of applications make use of identifying program features including
malware classification, software theft detection, plagiarism detection, and code
clone detection.

Malware classification is the process of determining if a program is malicious.
One approach to perform classification is to obtain a fingerprint of the malware
based on program feature extraction. This fingerprint creates an invariant signature
that can be used to identify evolutionary malware variants. For detection of
completely novel malware, program features can be extracted to create feature
vectors which can be subsequently used in machine learning algorithms and
statistical classification.

Software theft detection identifies unauthorized copying of a program in binary
form. An example of this is if a software library is illegally being used with regards
to its license. One approach to detect software theft is to identify birthmarks in the
software. A birthmark is a program feature or feature set that is invariant when the
software is illegally copied.

Plagiarism detection identifies similar or identical copying of source code. An
example of its use would be to detect student cheating in programming assignments. Plagiarism detection works by extracting program features that are
invariant when plagiarised. The program features are then detected in plagiarised
copies.

Code clone detection [1] seeks to identify duplicate fragments of code in a
source tree. The value in detecting code clones is that it is often bad software
development practice to have redundant or duplicate code fragments. By refac-
toring the code to eliminate clones, the software becomes easier to maintain and is
less likely to have bugs. Code clone detection works by identifying program
features for code fragments and identifying those features in other locations.

1.3 Motivation

Malware classification helps fight the threat of malicious software. Such malicious
software presents a significant challenge to modern desktop computing. According
to the Symantec Internet Threat Report [2], 499,811 new malware samples were
received in the second half of 2007. F-Secure additionally reported, "As much
malware [was] produced in 2007 as in the previous 20 years altogether" [3].
Detection of malware before it adversely affects computer systems is highly
desirable. Static detection of malware is still the dominant technique to secure
computer networks and systems against untrusted executable content.

Detecting malware variants improves signature based detection methods. The
size of signature databases is growing exponentially, and detecting entire families
of related malicious software can prevent the blowout in the number of stored

malware signatures. Detecting entire families of malware by using similarity measures instead of exact matching makes malware detection less fragile and more robust in the face of malware evolution and change.

Software theft detection is an important problem with serious consequences. In 2005, a federal court determined that the independent software vendor Compuserve be paid $140 million by IBM to license its software or $260 million to purchase its services because it was discovered that IBM products had illegitimately used code from Compuware without authorization [4]. The software theft problem is growing as the internet and software companies become more ubiquitous. For example, in SourceForge.net there were over 230,000 registered open source projects as of February 2009 [4]. Clearly, an automated approach to detecting software theft is the only way to scale with the problem.

Plagiarism detection is an important task to ensure that students do not cheat when submitting assignments. Without plagiarism detection systems, teachers rely on their own memory when marking. If the number of assignments is high, or the cheating occurs from previous years, or the assignments are divided between markers, plagiarism may go undetected. An automated approach to detecting plagiarism is therefore an important component in a teacher's arsenal against student cheating.

Code clone detection helps improve the maintainability of large software systems. Several studies have shown this that duplicated copy and paste fragments of code make code harder to maintain [5, 6]. This increases the cost of developing and maintaining software. Therefore, an effort to detect clones and refactor solutions leads to less cost in the software life cycle.

1.4 Problem Formulization

The static feature extraction problem is related to identifying invariant properties or approximations of the program.

Definition 1.1 Let r be a property for program p if for all possible executions r is true.

The software similarity problem is to determine if program p is a copy or derivative of program q. We use an extended definition based on software theft detection [7] (Fig. 1.1).

Definition 1.2 A program q is a copy of program p if it is exactly the same as p or it is the result of a semantic preserving transformation (e.g., obfuscation, recompilation, or optimisation) over p.

Definition 1.3 Programs p and q are similar if they are derived from the same works.

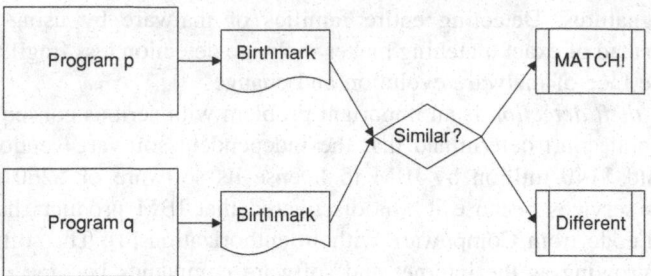

Fig. 1.1 The software similarity problem

Definition 1.4 Let p, q be programs. Let f be a method for extracting a set of characteristics extracted from p. We say $f(p)$ is a birthmark of p, only if both of the following conditions hold.

- $f(p)$ is obtained only from p itself
- Program q is a copy of $p \rightarrow f(p) = f(q)$

Definition 1.5 Let p, q be programs or program components. Let $f(p) \rightarrow a$ and $f(q) \rightarrow b$ be the birthmarks extracted from p and q. Let $s(a, b) \rightarrow [0,1]$ be a similarity function and a value $e < 1$. The birthmarking system is resilient if p and q are similar and $1 - s(a, b) < e$.

Definition 1.6 Let p and q be independently written programs. The software birthmarking system is credible if the system can discriminate between the two programs; that is $s(f(p), f(q)) < 1 - e$.

The software classification problem uses the birthmark feature to identify class membership of software.

Definition 1.7 Given a set of programs and their classes $\{(p_1, c_1), \ldots (p_n, c_n)\}$, the software classification function $c' = h(f(p))$ will yield a similar classification as close as possible to the true data set.

1.5 Problem Overview

The problem of software similarity and classification is approached by constructing a software birthmark for a program and then using a similarity function on that birthmark for comparisons. Program features are used to construct a birthmark. Different program features enable different birthmarks, so taxonomy of program features is useful. Different features have different properties which are better or worse at different qualities. A simple breakdown is to divide the features into syntactic and semantic properties. Syntax describes the structure or form of a program whereas the semantics describe the meaning of a program's instructions. Semantics are sometimes more useful than syntax when constructing birthmarks due to the fact that obfuscations and transformations applied to programs can modify that syntax while maintaining equivalent semantics. There are different approaches in extracting features such as extracting properties from execution of the program or extracting properties statically. For static analysis, program analysis techniques offer benefit. Decompilation is a specific program analysis technique that recovers high level source-like information from a binary. Decompilation offers some benefits to birthmark construction that we examine in this book. If program features are used to construct birthmarks, they must be represented in mathematical form. Different features are naturally represented using different structures. Once a birthmark is constructed, they can be compared using mathematical measures and metrics. The final result is a measure of similarity, or classification of birthmarks into classes using statistical machine learning.

1.6 Aims and Scope

The aim of this book is to survey software feature extraction, similarity and classification by investigating the principal concepts that constitute the construction of algorithms that tackle these problems. The intended purpose is to provide an opportunity for researchers and software engineers to understand the state-of-the-art and lay foundation for the creation of extended works to extract software features, determine software similarity, and perform software classification.

The scope of this book is limited to the theory of software feature extraction, similarity, and classification. It has significant applications and four of those examined by this book are:

- Malware Classification
- Software Theft Detection
- Plagiarism Detection
- Software Clone Detection

For applications that fall outside of this scope, readers are advised to find other relevant sources and references.

1.7 Book Organization

The structure of this book is as follows:

- Chapter 2 gives taxonomy of program features.

- Chapter 3 examines program obfuscations and transformations that may affect the quality of fingerprinting software and extracting features.
- Chapter 4 examines formal methods and static techniques to extract features whether it is from parsing source code or performing static analysis.
- Chapter 5 provides a review of the static technique of analysing binaries and performing decompilation, which both can be used also to extract software features.
- Chapter 6 provides an alternative to static feature extraction by using dynamic analysis.
- Chapter 7 provides an analysis of feature extraction.
- Chapter 8 covers how software birthmarks are compared to result in similarity and distance measures.
- Chapter 9 covers software similarity searching and classification.
- Chapter 10 evaluates literature in malware classification, software theft detection, plagiarism detection, and code clone detection. The evaluation identifies the techniques used in the context of the framework presented in this survey.
- Chapter 11 examines future trends and concludes the book.

References

1. Roy CK, Cordy JR (2007) A survey on software clone detection research. Queen's School of Computing TR 541:115
2. Symantec (2008) Symantec internet security threat report: Volume XII. Symantec
3. F-Secure (2007) F-Secure reports amount of malware grew by 100% during 2007
4. Wang X, Jhi Y-C, Zhu S, Liu P (2009) Behavior based software theft detection. Paper presented at the proceedings of the 16th ACM conference on computer and communications security, Chicago
5. Baker BS (1995) On finding duplication and near-duplication in large software systems. In: Proceedings of the second working conference on reverse engineering (WCRE '95). Published by the IEEE Computer Society, p 86
6. Johnson JH (1993) Identifying redundancy in source code using fingerprints. In: Proceedings of the 1993 conference of the centre for advanced studies on collaborative research (CASCON '93). IBM Press, pp 171–183
7. Tamada H, Okamoto K, Nakamura M, Monden A, Matsumoto K (2004) Dynamic software birthmarks to detect the theft of windows applications. In: International symposium on future software technology (ISFST 2004)

Chapter 2
Taxonomy of Program Features

Abstract All programs have common features and abstractions which are used to create birthmarks. Features can be divided into syntactic and semantic groups. Syntactic features concern themselves with program structure and program form. Semantic features examine the meaning of the program. In this chapter we examine those syntactic and semantic features of programs. Syntactic Features include: (1) Raw Code, (2) Abstract Syntax Trees, (3) Variables, (4) Pointers, (5) Instructions, (6) Basic Blocks, (7) Procedures, (8) Control Flow Graphs, (9) Call Graphs, and (10) Object Inheritances and Dependencies. Semantic features include: (1) API Calls, (2) Data Flow, (3) Procedure Dependence Graphs, and (4) System Dependence Graphs.

Keywords Program features · Raw code · Abstract syntax tree · Variables · Pointer · Instruction · Basic block · Procedure · Control flow graph · Call graph · Object inheritance · Object dependence · API call · Data flow · Procedure dependence graph · System dependence graph

2.1 Syntactic Features

2.1.1 Raw Code

The raw code of the program can be analysed directly. For source code this is the textual stream, possibly normalized by removing comments and whitespace. For binaries, the raw code is the byte sequences (Fig. 2.1).

Definition 2.1 Let $\sum$ be an alphabet of symbols. The raw code of program p is defined by the function r that evaluates to a string over the alphabet.

S. Cesare and Y. Xiang, *Software Similarity and Classification*,
SpringerBriefs in Computer Science, DOI: 10.1007/978-1-4471-2909-7_2,
© The Author(s) 2012

```
00000000 00000000 00000000 00000000  ..............
00000000 00000000 00000000 00000000  ..............
00000000 00000000 00000000 00000000  ..............
63796767 63635f73 2d312e64 6c6c005f  cyggcc_s-1.dll._
5f726567 69737465 725f6672 616d655f  _register_frame_
696e666f 00637967 67636a2d 392e646c  info.cyggcj-9.dl
6c005f4a 765f5265 67697374 6572436c  l._Jv_RegisterCl
61737365 73005f5f 64657265 67697374  asses.__deregist
65725f66 72616d65 5f696e66 6f000000  er_frame_info...
55736167 653a2025 73205b4f 5054494f  Usage: %s [OPTIO
```

```
 *
 * -THE SOFTWARE IS PROVIDED "AS-IS", WITHOUT ANY
WARRANTIES,
 * EXPRESSED OR IMPLIED.  USE IT AT YOUR OWN RISK.
 *************************************************************
 *************/
// -*- c++ -*-
#ifndef _cvcl__include__c_interface_h_
#define _cvcl__include__c_interface_h_
```

Fig. 2.1 Raw code for a binary (*left*) and source code (*right*)

Fig. 2.2 An abstract syntax tree (*AST*)

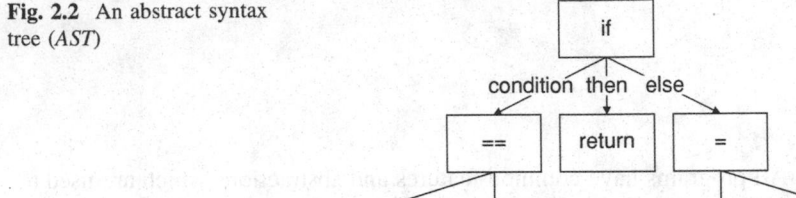

$$r : P \rightarrow S$$
$$p \rightarrow s, s \in \sum *$$

2.1.2 Abstract Syntax Trees

Abstract syntax trees (AST) examine the syntax of source code and construct a tree representing the syntactical structure. For binaries, decompilation is required to reconstruct an abstract syntax tree (Fig. 2.2).

2.1.3 Variables

Variables represent the state of data. Programs typically maintain separate regions of memory for different classes of data handled by the run time environment. Run times may separate the stack from the heap to store data. The stack is used for local variables in a procedure and survives for the scope of that procedure or activation record. The run time creates a stack segment to achieve this outcome. In contrast, the heap is used for dynamically generated memory. Global variables conceptually belong to a different region than the heap, but for practical purposes are normally grouped together at run time in a data segment (Fig. 2.2).

Fig. 2.3 Typical pointer operations

p = malloc
*p = q
p = *q
p = &q
p = q

2.1.4 Pointers

Pointers are a type of variable that contain links or pointers to other variables. Pointers can be dereferenced, which allows for referencing the data the pointer is pointing to. Pointers may allow pointer arithmetic to be performed which allows for such operations as incrementing the value of a pointer. Some languages allow seemingly arbitrary pointer arithmetic, while other languages heavily restrict their use. Restricting pointer arithmetic allows for easier automated analysis (Fig. 2.3).

2.1.5 Instructions

Instructions capture the basic unit of computation. Computations can include such things as unary and binary operations, procedure or library calls. An instruction is defined by its operand and opcodes.

Definition 2.2 Let I be set of all instructions such that $I = \{(\text{opcode}, \text{operand}_1, \ldots, \text{operand}_n)\}$

Definition 2.3 Let InstrSequence be a string of instructions such that $InstrSequence \in \sum *, \sum = I$

2.1.5.1 Assembly

Assembly is a low level instruction format that can be executed on the native processing unit. It consists of opcodes which describe the type of operation to perform, and operands which are the arguments or parameters. Assembly language can be roughly divided into Complex Instruction Set Computing (CISC) architectures, or Reduced Instruction Set Architectures (RISC). RISC architectures favour simplified and small instruction sets while CISC architectures favour a rich and large instruction set. ×86 is the dominant architecture for personal computing and is a CISC based architecture (Fig. 2.4).

2.1.5.2 Intermediate Representations

Instructions can be abstracted into intermediate representations. A common representation is Three-Address-Code which consists of three operands and one opcode. Typically, two fixed operands are inputs and the remaining operand is the

```
8d 4c 24 04          lea    0x4(%esp),%ecx         lea    0x4(%esp),%ecx
83 e4 f0             and    $0xfffffff0,%esp        and    $0xfffffff0,%esp
ff 71 fc             pushl  -0x4(%ecx)              pushl  -0x4(%ecx)
55                   push   %ebp                    push   %ebp
89 e5                mov    %esp,%ebp               mov    %esp,%ebp
51                   push   %ecx                    push   %ecx
83 ec 24             sub    $0x24,%esp              sub    $0x24,%esp
e8 6a 00 00 00       call   4011b0 <__main>         call   4011b0 <__main>
c7 45 f8 00 00 00 00 movl   $0x0,-0x8(%ebp)         movl   $0x0,-0x8(%ebp)
eb 10                jmp    40115f <_main+0x2f>     jmp    40115f <_main+0x2f>
c7 04 24 a0 20 40 00 movl   $0x4020a0,(%esp)
e8 5d 00 00 00       call   4011b8 <_puts>          movl   $0x4020a0,(%esp)
83 45 f8 01          addl   $0x1,-0x8(%ebp)         call   4011b8 <_puts>
83 7d f8 09          cmpl   $0x9,-0x8(%ebp)         addl   $0x1,-0x8(%ebp)
7e ea                jle    40114f <_main+0x1f>
83 c4 24             add    $0x24,%esp              cmpl   $0x9,-0x8(%ebp)
59                   pop    %ecx                    jle    40114f <_main+0x1f>
5d                   pop    %ebp
8d 61 fc             lea    -0x4(%ecx),%esp
c3                   ret                            add    $0x24,%esp
                                                    pop    %ecx
                                                    pop    %ebp
                                                    lea    -0x4(%ecx),%esp
                                                    ret
```

Fig. 2.4 Assembly instructions and basic blocks

output. For unary operations, the extra operands are ignored. Using intermediate representation has the advantage of normalizing a complex instruction set into a series of simpler standardized operations.

Definition 2.4 Let TAC = (opcode, operand$_1$, operand$_2$, operand$_3$)

2.1.6 Basic Blocks

A basic block is a sequence of instructions that satisfy the following conditions:

- Execution flow can only enter the basic block through the first instruction.
- Execution flow can only exit the block at the last instruction.

A basic block can also be represented as s directed cyclic graph showing the data dependencies between instructions.

Definition 2.5 Let InstrSequence(b) be a string of instructions such that $InstrSequence \in \sum *, \sum = I$ for basic block b

2.1.7 Procedures

Procedures and functions are found in structured programming which allows for making modular maintainable code. A program uses a set of procedures $F = procedures\ (p) = \{f_1, \ldots, f_n\}$.

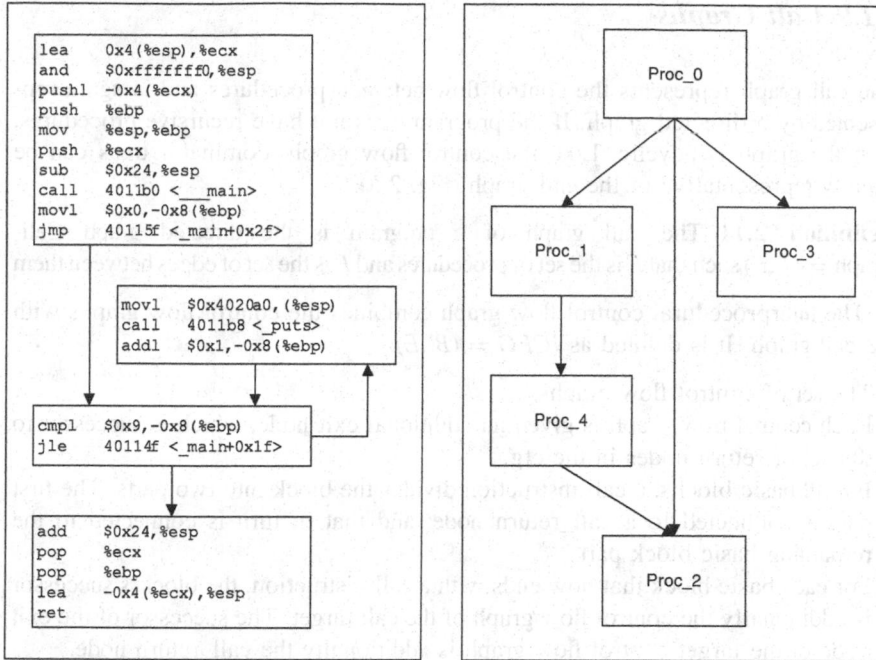

Fig. 2.5 A control flow graph (*left*) and a call graph (*right*)

2.1.8 Control Flow Graphs

The control flow graph is a directed graph representing the possible flow of execution within a procedure. The nodes in the graph represent basic blocks (Fig. 2.5).

Definition 2.6 The control flow graph of procedure f is the directed graph $C = (B,E)$ such that B is the set of basic blocks and E is the set of edges between them

Alternative representations of control flow are possible using graphs such as dominator trees or control dependency graphs.

Definition 2.7 d dom n or node d dominates a node n if every path from the start node to n must go through d

Definition 2.8 A node d strictly dominates a node n if d dominates n and d does not equal n

Definition 2.9 The immediate dominator or idom of a node n is the node that strictly dominates n but does not strictly dominate any other node that strictly dominate n

Definition 2.10 A dominator tree is a tree where each node's children are those nodes it immediately dominates

2.1.9 Call Graphs

The call graph represents the control flow between procedures and is again represented by a directed graph. If the program does not have recursive procedures, then the graph is acyclic. Like the control flow graph, dominator trees can be equally representative of the call graph (Fig. 2.5).

Definition 2.11 The call graph of a program is the directed graph Call-Graph $= (F,E)$ such that F is the set of procedures and E is the set of edges between them

The interprocedural control flow graph combines the control flow graphs with the call graph. It is defined as $ICFG = (B',E)$:

- The set of control flow graphs.
- Each control flow graph is given an additional exit node, which is successor to the set of return nodes in the cfg.
- For all basic blocks, a call instruction divides the block into two parts. The first part is connected to a call_return node, and that in turn is connected to the remaining basic block part.
- For each basic block that now ends with a call instruction, the block's successor is additionally the control flow graph of the call target. The successor of the exit node of the target control flow graph is additionally the call_return node.

2.1.10 Object Inheritances and Dependencies

Objects come from object oriented languages which group procedures (known as methods) and data into modular units. Objects are related to other objects via inheritance of their functionality.

2.2 Semantic Features

2.2.1 API Calls

API calls represent calls to libraries and other imports.

2.2.2 Data Flow

Data flow statically represents the data at run time entering and leaving each basic block. Many types of data flow analyses [1] are possible including reaching definitions, liveness, available expressions, and very busy expressions.

2.2.3 Procedure Dependence Graphs

The control dependencies and data dependencies of a procedure can be represented in a single graph using a procedure dependence graph [2].

2.2.4 System Dependence Graph

The system dependence graph combines the set of procedure dependency graphs of each procedure into a unified representation.

2.3 Taxonomy of Features in Program Binaries

Programs may begin as source code, but are typically compiled into a target binary for execution on the native platform or in another run time environment. The target binary is a container for all the information necessary for its execution in the target environment. This container is known as the object file format [3].

2.3.1 Object File Formats

Object File Formats contain five types of data:

- Headers.
- Object Code.
- Symbols.
- Debugging Information.
- Relocations.

Most modern object files also contain:

- Dynamic Linking Information.

2.3.2 Headers

The object file format is often described by a variety of headers. Headers may be used to define where the object code, symbols, debugging information, etc., is present in the binary.

2.3.3 Object Code

Object code contains the code and data of the program. For native executables the object code can consist of assembly or machine code. For object file formats such as Java class files, the object code contains byte code which is the instruction set architecture of the Java Virtual Machine.

2.3.4 Symbols

Parts of the code, data and binary may be associated with symbolic names. These associations are organized and stored in a Symbol Table.

2.3.5 Debugging Information

The binary may contain debugging information such as line numbers of source code associated with object code, or naming of information for different codes or data.

2.3.6 Relocations

If the binary has not been associated with a specific load address at compile time, the binary may need to be link edited at runtime. Relocations or fixups contain the necessary information to bind the object code to a specific load address.

2.3.7 Dynamic Linking Information

If the binary requires the use of external libraries, then the names of the required library functions must be present. Likewise, if the binary's functions are being exported as a library, then this information must also be present.

2.4 Case Studies

2.4.1 Portable Executable

The Portable Executable (PE) format [4] is the native object file format for the Windows family of operating systems. It is a modern file format which can contain

```
/bin/ls:      file format pei-i386
architecture: i386, flags 0x00000102:
EXEC_P, D_PAGED
start address 0x00401000
Sections:
Idx Name            Size      VMA       LMA       File off  Algn
  0 .text           00019528  00401000  00401000  00000400  2**4
                    CONTENTS, ALLOC, LOAD, READONLY, CODE, DATA
  1 .data           00004be4  0041b000  0041b000  00019a00  2**5
                    CONTENTS, ALLOC, LOAD, DATA
  2 .eh_frame       00000004  00420000  00420000  0001e600  2**2
                    CONTENTS, ALLOC, LOAD, DATA
  3 .bss            0000103c  00421000  00421000  00000000  2**3
                    ALLOC
  4 .idata          00000ddc  00423000  00423000  0001e800  2**2
                    CONTENTS, ALLOC, LOAD, DATA
```

Fig. 2.6 The output of objdump on a PE executable

all the information we have described in this section. It is identified by a series of magic bytes in its headers. Object code is defined in PE sections and an Import Address Table allows for dynamic linking.

2.4.2 Executable and Linking Format

The Executable and Linking Format [5] is the object file format in use on Linux and other operating systems. It replaced the previous a.out object file format in Linux. The a.out object file format did not natively support dynamic linking and ELF brought a much more modern format to Linux and enabled the transition to shared libraries using dynamic linking. An ELF binary is identified by a magic sequence in its header. There are three types of ELF object files (Fig. 2.6).

• Executable Objects.
• Relocatable Objects.
• Dynamic Objects.

Executable objects have been linked and bound to an address. Relocatable objects have not been bound to a load address and require linking. Dynamic objects have both a relocatable view and an executable view—shared libraries use this format.

Dynamic linking is slightly different to the PE format and uses a Global Offset Table (GOT) and a stub call to the runtime linker to resolve imports.

2.4.3 Java Class File

Java class files [6] contain object code in sections defined in the file's headers. The object code is in the instruction format for execution on the Java Virtual Machine. Like the previous object file format, a sequence of marker bytes (the magic bytes) in the header identifies the file format.

References

1. Aho AV, Sethi R, Ullman JD (1986) Compilers: principles, techniques, and tools. Addison-Wesley, Reading MA
2. Ferrante J, Ottenstein KJ, Warren JD (1987) The program dependence graph and its use in optimization. ACM Trans Program Lang Syst (TOPLAS) 9(3):319–349
3. Levine JR (2000) Linkers and loaders. Morgan Kaufmann Pub, Massachusetts
4. Pietrek M (2002) Inside windows-an in-depth look into the Win32 portable executable file format. MSDN magazine, pp 80–92
5. Standard TI (1995) Executable and linking format (ELF) specification version 1.2. In: TIS committee, May
6. Lindholm T, Yellin F (1999) Java virtual machine specification. Addison-Wesley Longman Publishing Co., Inc., Boston

Chapter 3
Program Transformations and Obfuscations

Abstract Software feature extraction must cope with transformations that are intended to obscure, evolve, or rewrite the program. For example, malware polymorphism and metamorphism are transformations applied to the malicious code to evade signature detection. Robust signatures must identify the invariant birthmarks under these transformations. This chapter focuses on analysing these types of program transformations and obfuscations including compiler optimsations, recompilation, plagiarism, software theft, derivative works, malware packing, malware polymorphism and malware metamorphism.

Keywords Program obfuscation · Compiler optimisation · Code packing · Polymorphism · Metamorphism

3.1 Compiler Optimisation and Recompilation

Compiler optimisations and recompilation are semantic preserving transformations. These transformations rewrite the program but do not alter the behavioural properties of the software. Compiler optimisations make feature extraction more difficult. Even very minor changes to a program's source code can result in significant changes to the program's instruction stream once recompiled.

Many compiler optimisations are possible. We examine some in this section. Typical classes of code optimisation that may affect the birthmarks and feature extraction are:

- Instruction Reordering
- Loop Invariant Code Motion
- Code Fusion
- Function Inlining
- Loop Unrolling

S. Cesare and Y. Xiang, *Software Similarity and Classification*,
SpringerBriefs in Computer Science, DOI: 10.1007/978-1-4471-2909-7_3,
© The Author(s) 2012

- Branch/Loop Inversion
- Strength Reduction
- Algebraic Identities
- Register Assignment

3.1.1 Instruction Reordering

Instructions can be reordered or scheduled in such a way that they are semantically equivalent but perform faster due to caching. To determine if instructions inside a basic block can be reordered, a directed acyclic graph can be drawn of the data dependencies. Only instructions that have data dependencies between each other require strict ordering between those instructions.

3.1.2 Loop Invariant Code Motion

Code that is inside a loop may be moved to outside the loop if no semantic change occurs. This improves the efficiency of the code.

3.1.3 Code Fusion

Code inside loops in sequence can be fused into a single loop.

3.1.4 Function Inlining

Functions can be inlined to improve performance. Inlining a function means that a clone or copy of that function replaces the function call. This means that a function call is avoided and therefore improves performance.

3.1.5 Loop Unrolling

It can improve efficiency to unroll the loop by duplicating the loop body and termination condition.

3.1.6 Branch/Loop Inversion

Branching on equality or non equality can be inverted and may improve efficiency in some cases.

3.1.7 Strength Reduction

Strength reduction replaces expensive operations with equivalent but less expensive operations.

3.1.8 Algebraic Identities

Algebraic identities take note that some expressions are algebraically equivalent to other less expensive operations. For example, x + 0 is equivalent to the less expensive expression x.

3.1.9 Register Reassignment

Register allocation is the process of assigning specific registers to instructions. The assignment of these registers can change while maintaining semantically equivalent code.

3.2 Program Obfuscation

Program obfuscation obscures the workings of a program [1].

Definition 3.1 Let $P \xrightarrow{T} P'$ be a transformation of a source program P into a target program P'. $P \xrightarrow{T} P'$ is an obfuscating transformation, if P and P' have the same observable behaviour. More precisely, in order for $P \xrightarrow{T} P'$ to be a legal obfuscating transformation the following conditions must hold:

- If P fails to terminate or terminates with an error condition, then P' may or may not terminate.
- Otherwise, P' must terminate and produce the same output as P.

3.3 Plagiarism, Software Theft, and Derivative Works

An incomplete list of source code plagiarism techniques is described in [2]. The authors state that such a list is never ending, so a comprehensive list is impossible. Nevertheless, they identified the following forms of plagiarism:

- Lexical Changes

  - Comments can be reworded, added and omitted.
  - Formatting can be changed.
  - Identifier names can be modified.
  - Line numbers can be changed (e.g., in Fortran programs).

- Structural Changes

  - Loops can be replaced (e.g., replacing a while loop with a for loop).
  - Nested if statements can be replaced by case statements and vice versa.
  - Statement order can be changed.
  - Procedures can be replaced by functions (e.g., in Pascal).
  - Procedures may be inlined.
  - Ordering of operands may be changed (e.g., x < y becomes x > = y).

3.3.1 Semantic Changes

An extension to syntactic changes is that of semantic changes where the new variant is a derived work of the original malware. Semantic changes occur due to the software authors modifying the original source code or functionality. This can occur to a natural evolution of the software during its development life cycle. Additionally, it can occur when a software author reuses existing code in a new program instance.

3.3.2 Code Insertion

Code insertion occurs when new functionality is added to the malware.

3.3.3 Code Deletion

Code deletion occurs when functionality is removed from the malware.

3.3.4 Code Substitution

Code substitution occurs when functionality in the malware is replaced by an alternative algorithm or code.

3.3.5 Code Transposition

Code transposition occurs when specific code and functionality of the malware is removed from its initial location and inserted into a semantically different location in the malware.

3.4 Malware Packing, Polymorphism, and Metamorphism

The two categories of malware obfuscation are syntactic and semantic changes. Semantic changes include those described for plagiarism and software theft. A syntactic polymorphic malware technique is a method that changes the syntactic structure of the malware [3]. Though the syntactic structure changes in polymorphic malware, the malware semantically remains identical. The technique is predominantly used to evade byte level signature based detection and classification that is routinely employed by traditional Antivirus. Polymorphism borrows many of the techniques from the field of program obfuscation.

Polymorphism is sometimes described by the similar term of metamorphism. In that usage it is used to describe the automated syntactic mutation of the malware's code and instructions. Under such terminology, polymorphism is used to describe syntactic mutation of limited parts of the malware's instruction content. The remaining parts of the malware are encoded at the byte level without regard to the instruction syntax or semantics. In this book we treat polymorphism and metamorphism as identical to each other.

Syntactic malware obfuscations and transformations include:

* Dead Code Insertion
* Instruction Substitution
* Variable Renaming
* Code Reordering
* Branch Inversion and Flipping
* Opaque Predicate Insertion
* Code Packing

3.4.1 Dead Code Insertion

Dead code is also known as junk code and a semantic nop [3]. Dead code is semantically equivalent to a nil operation. Insertion of this type of code has no semantic impact on the malware. The insertion increases the size of the malware and modifies the byte and instruction level content of the malware (Fig. 3.1).

Fig. 3.1 A semantic nop

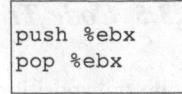

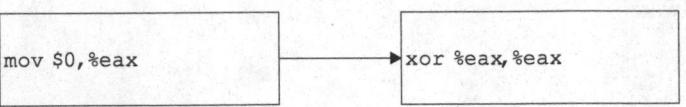

Fig. 3.2 Instruction substituion

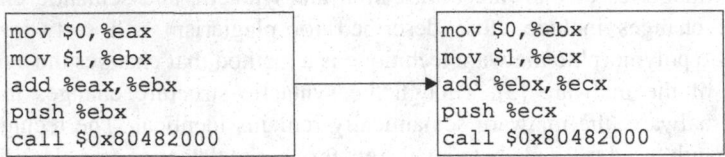

Fig. 3.3 Register reassignment

3.4.2 Instruction Substitution

Instruction substitution replaces specific instructions or sequences of instructions with semantically equivalent, but differing instructions and instruction sequences. The size of the malware may grow or shrink in this procedure (Fig. 3.2).

3.4.3 Variable Renaming

Variable renaming [4] and the associated technique of register reassignment alters the use of variables and registers in a sequence of code such that the instructions are semantically equivalent but use different variables and registers when compared to the original code (Fig. 3.3).

3.4.4 Code Reordering

Code reordering [4] changes the syntactic order of the code in the malware [3]. The actual or semantic execution path of the program does not change. However, the syntactic order as present in the malware image is altered. Code reordering includes the techniques of branch obfuscation, branch inversion, branch flipping, and the use of opaque predicates.

Fig. 3.4 An indirect branch

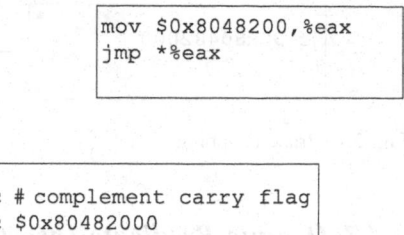

```
mov $0x8048200,%eax
jmp *%eax
```

```
jc $0x80482000
```
→
```
cmc # complement carry flag
jnc $0x80482000
```

Fig. 3.5 Branch inversion

3.4.5 Branch Obfuscation

Branch obfuscation attempts to hide the target of a branch instruction. Examples include the use of Structured Exception Handling (SEH) on the Microsoft Windows platform. The use of SEH to obscure control flow is common in modern malware. Similar techniques involve indirect branching. Indirect branching uses data content as the target of a branch. This translates control flow identification into a harder data flow analysis problem. The use of a branch function [5] extends this approach and dispatches multiple branches through a single routine. The main purpose of branch obfuscation is to make the static analysis of the malware by an analyst or automated system harder to perform (Fig. 3.4).

3.4.6 Branch Inversion and Flipping

Branch inversion inverts the branch condition in conditional branches. Whereas the branch may originally transfer control when the condition is true, branch inversion alters the condition to branch when false. To maintain the original semantics of the program the branch instruction is also inverted. For example, a branch on condition true statement can be changed to a branch on condition false statement. Additionally, the condition being tested would also be inverted. Branch inversion is effectively a form of instruction substitution on control flow statements.

Branch flipping [5] is a similar technique to branch inversion and rewrites the branch instruction by substituting it with semantically equivalent code with different control flow properties. For example, if the original code is to branch on condition true then the new code branches on condition false to the original fall-through instruction. The new fall-through instruction then unconditionally branches to the original conditional branch target (Figs. 3.5 and 3.6).

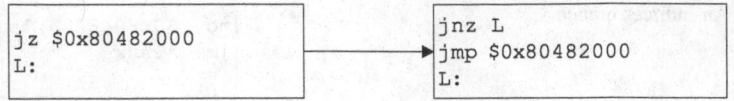

Fig. 3.6 Branch flipping

3.4.7 Opaque Predicate Insertion

An opaque predicate [5] is a predicate that always evaluates to the same result. An opaque predicate is constructed so that it is difficult for an analyst or automated analysis to know the predicate result. Opaque predicates can be used to insert superfluous branching in the malware's control flow. They can also be used to assign variables values which are hard to determine statically. The use of opaque predicates is primarily for code obfuscation, and to prevent understanding by an analyst or automated static analysis.

3.4.8 Malware Obfuscation Using Code Packing

Code packing [6, 7] is the dominant technique used to obfuscate malware and hinder an analyst's understanding of the malware's intent. In one month during 2007, 79% of identified malware from a commercial Antivirus vendor was found to be packed [8]. Additionally, almost 50% of new malware in 2006 were repacked versions of existing malware [9].

Code packing, in addition to obfuscating the understanding of the malware by an analyst, is also used by malware to evade an Antivirus system's detection. Polypack [10] evaluated the effectiveness of code packing against Antivirus detection by providing a service to pack malware using a variety of code packing tools. Antivirus systems often have the capabilities of unpacking known code packing tools, and unpacking unknown tools has also had commercial interest [11]. However, Polypack demonstrated that packing can be an effective tool to defeat an Antivirus system with many commercial malware detection systems failing to identify the packed versions of existing malware.

Code packing is used in the majority of malware, but code packing also serves to provide compression and software protection for the intellectual property contained in a program. It is not necessarily advantageous to flag all occurrences of code packing as being indicative of malicious activity. Code packing tools are freely available [12] and commercially sold to the public as legitimate software [13]. For this reason, unpacking of packed programs provides benefit. It is advisable to determine if the packed contents are malicious, rather than identifying only the fact that unknown contents are packed.

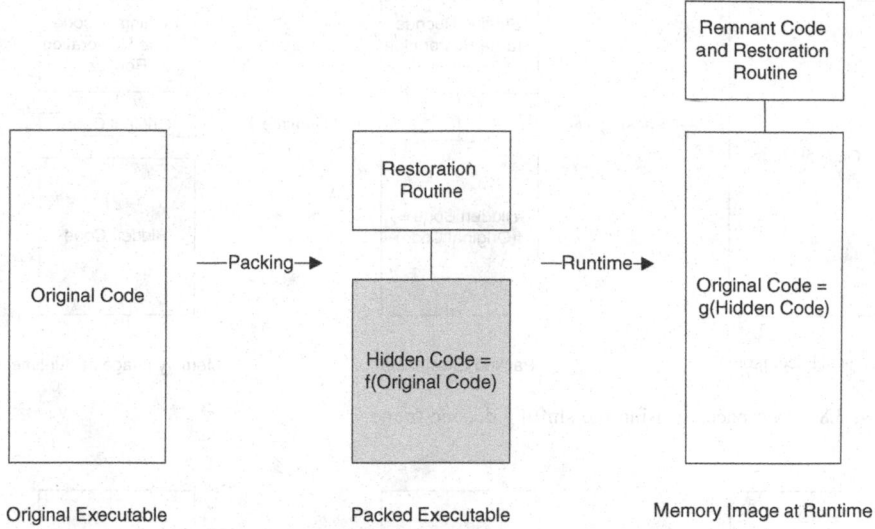

Fig. 3.7 The traditional code packing transformation

3.4.9 Traditional Code Packing

The most common method of code packing is described in [6]. Malware employing this method of code packing transforms executable code into data as a post-processing stage in the malware development cycle. This transformation may perform compression or encryption, hindering an analyst's understanding of the malware when using static analysis. At runtime, the data, or hidden code, is restored to its original executable form through dynamic code generation using an associated restoration routine [14]. Execution then resumes as normal to the original entry point. The original entry point marks the entry point of the original malware, before the code packing transformation is applied. Execution of the malware, once the restoration routine is complete and control is transferred to the original entry point, is transparent to the fact that code packing and restoration had been performed. A malware may have the code packing transformation applied more than once. After the restoration routine of one packing transformation has been applied, control may transfer another packed layer. The original entry point is derived from the last such layer. The process of this form of malware packing is shown in Fig. 3.7.

3.4.10 Shifting Decode Frame

An extension to traditional code packing is to maintain as much of the packed image in an encrypted form at run-time. During execution of the malware, blocks of memory can be decrypted as needed and subsequently re-encrypted to prevent an analyst or

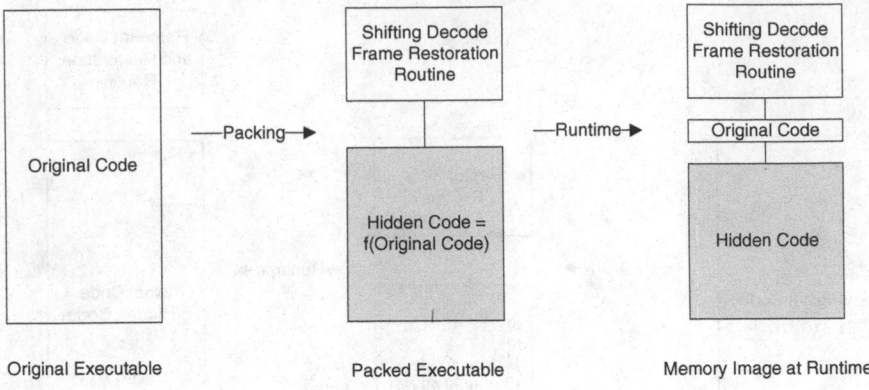

Fig. 3.8 Code packing using the shifting decode frame

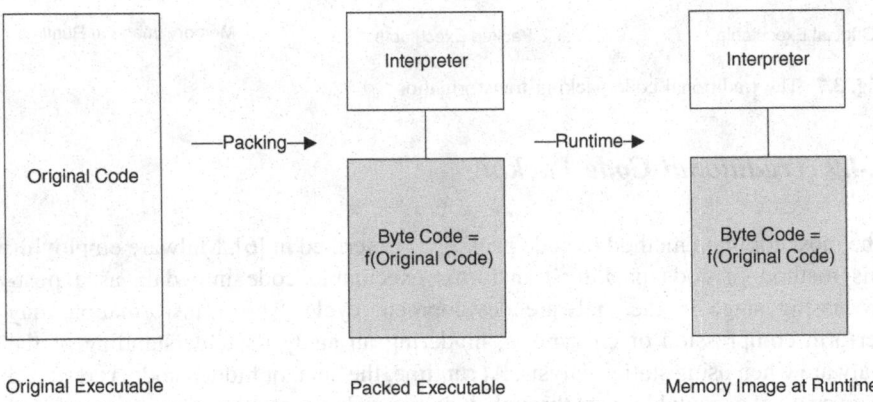

Fig. 3.9 Code packing using instruction virtualization

automated system from having access to all the hidden code at any single moment in time. This technique is known as the shifting decode frame [15]. The granularity of encryption can occur at the page level, the basic block level, and the instruction level. This type of code packing is not often used in wild malware, and in practice, traditional code packing and instruction virtualization are the dominant techniques used in real malware. The process of this form of malware packing is shown in Fig. 3.8.

3.4.11 Instruction Virtualization and Malware Emulators

Code packing may employ the use of instruction virtualization also known as a malware emulator [7]. An emulator used by a malware should not be confused with an emulator used for automated unpacking of the malware. This type of code packing transformation employing an emulator is used in a minority of malware. In this form of code packing, packing translates the original native code into a byte-code which is subsequently emulated by the malware at run-time. Using this form of code packing, the hidden code in its original form is never revealed. The process of this form of malware packing is shown in Fig. 3.9.

3.5 Features under Program Transformations

Program features may change under program transformations and obfuscation. The challenge then is in choosing features which remain invariant under these conditions. The raw or byte level content deals poorly with program transformations. Small changes in high level source code may result in large changes in the raw content. Instruction level content is also prone to large changes under transformations such as when registers are reassigned or the instruction stream is modified. Control flow is more invariant than most syntactic features and can be a good choice. At a source code level, program and system dependency graphs have been popular. The APIs used by a program represent a good choice and have been widely used in behavioural analysis of malware. For static analysis of malware, the malware must be unpacked to reveal its hidden code. Unpacking of malware is not addressed in this book.

References

1. Collberg C, Thomborson C, Low D (1997) A taxonomy of obfuscating transformations. Department of computer science, The University of Auckland, New Zealand
2. Joy M, Luck M (1999) Plagiarism in programming assignments. Education, IEEE transactions on 42 (2):129–133
3. Christodorescu M, Kinder J, Jha S, Katzenbeisser S, Veith H (2005) Malware normalization. University of Wisconsin, Madison
4. Mihai C, Somesh J (2004) Testing malware detectors. Paper presented at the proceedings of the 2004 ACM SIGSOFT international symposium on software testing and analysis, Boston
5. Cullen L, Saumya D (2003) Obfuscation of executable code to improve resistance to static disassembly. Paper presented at the Proceedings of the 10th ACM conference on computer and communications security, Washington
6. Royal P, Halpin M, Dagon D, Edmonds R, Lee W (2006) Polyunpack: automating the hidden-code extraction of unpack-executing malware. In: Computer security applications conference, pp 289–300
7. Sharif M, Lanzi A, Giffin J, Lee W (2009) Rotalume: a tool for automatic reverse engineering of malware emulators. Paper presented at the proceedings of the 30th IEEE symposium on security and privacy
8. Panda Research (2007) Mal(ware)formation statistics–Panda Research Blog
9. Stepan A (2006) Improving proactive detection of packed malware. In: Virus Bulletin Conference
10. Oberheide J, Bailey M, Jahanian F (2009) Polypack. In: USENIX workshop on offensive technologies (WOOT '09), Montreal
11. Graf T (2005) Generic unpacking: How to handle modified or unknown PE compression engines. Paper presented at the Virus Bulletin Conference

12. UPX: the Ultimate Packer for eXecutables (2010) http://upx.sourceforge.net/. Accessed 6 April 2010
13. Themida (2010) http://www.themida.com/. Accessed 6 April 2010
14. Kang MG, Poosankam P, Yin H (2007) Renovo: a hidden code extractor for packed executables. In: Workshop on recurring malcode, pp 46–53
15. Boehne L (2008) Pandora's Bochs: automatic unpacking of malware. University of Mannheim

Chapter 4
Formal Methods of Program Analysis

Abstract Feature extraction is a necessary component to construct a birthmark, show similarity and classify a program as belonging to a particular class. Program analysis is an important component in feature extraction. The analysis reveals information on the syntax, semantics, and behaviour of the program being inspected. This chapter focuses on formal methods of program analysis which can be used for the purpose of property and feature extraction.

Keywords Lexical analysis · Parsing · Intermediate representation · Formal semantics · Theorem proving · Model checking · Data flow analysis · Static program analysis

4.1 Static Feature Extraction

The majority of formal methods we will examine in this chapter are based on analysing a static view of a program without performing execution of it. A number of possible choices exist to perform feature extraction statically from a program. There is some equivalence between source code and binary feature extraction, however differences also exist.

The possible stages to extract static features from source code are:

- Raw Code Analysis
- Lexical Analysis
- Parsing
- Static Program Analysis

S. Cesare and Y. Xiang, *Software Similarity and Classification*,
SpringerBriefs in Computer Science, DOI: 10.1007/978-1-4471-2909-7_4,
© The Author(s) 2012

Fig. 4.1 Implementation of
lexical analysis

```
digit          [0-9]
letter         [a-zA-Z]

%%
"<="                    { return LEQ;          }
">="                    { return GEQ;          }
"begin"                 { return BEGINSYM;     }
"call"                  { return CALLSYM;      }
"const"                 { return CONSTSYM;     }
"do"                    { return DOSYM;        }
"end"                   { return ENDSYM;       }
```

For binary only software, analyses can be divided into:

- Raw Code Analysis
- Object File Parsing
- Static Program Analysis of Binaries
- Decompilation

Static program analysis is an approximation of program behaviour. For an analysis to be sound, then no behaviour should be omitted. For an analysis to be precise, the over-approximation should be close to the actual behaviour. This over approximation leads to false positives in the case of bug detection, or conservation optimisations in the case of compiler techniques. A perfectly precise analysis is undecidable due to Rice's theorem [1], however even without perfect precision the results are still practical and useful.

4.2 Formal Syntax and Lexical Analysis

Lexical analysis is the process of producing a sequence of tokens given a sequence of characters. Lexical analysis is performed before parsing. The parser uses the tokens generated from the lexical analysis (Fig. 4.1).

4.3 Parsing

Definition 4.1 A context-free grammar G is defined by the 4-tuple:
$\quad G = (V, \Sigma, R, S)$ where
V   is a finite set of non terminal variables,
Σ   is a finite set of terminals (Fig. 4.2),
R   is a finite set of rules or productions of the grammar,
S   is the start variable.

```
input:
        expr { ((SParserParam*)data)->expression = $1; }
        ;
  expr:
        expr TOKEN_PLUS expr { $$=createOperation( ePLUS, $1, $3 ); }
      | expr TOKEN_MULTIPLY expr { $$=createOperation( eMULTIPLY, $1, $3 ); }
      | TOKEN_LPAREN expr TOKEN_RPAREN { $$=$2; }
      | TOKEN_NUMBER { $$ = createNumber($1); }
  ;
```

Fig. 4.2 Implementation of parsing

Rules are of the form $V \rightarrow w$ where V is a non terminal symbol and w is a string of terminals and/or non terminals.

Context-free grammars are the basis for recognizing and representing programming languages in source code. However, in practice, a number of widely used languages such as C++ are not strictly context-free in all cases.

The process of parsing in static analysis is to transform source code into a concrete or abstract syntax tree.

4.4 Intermediate Representations

4.4.1 Intermediate Code Generation

The process of code generation is typically performed by traversing the abstract syntax tree and generating intermediate code for each unit in the tree.

4.4.2 Abstract Machines

The intermediate language used for the intermediate code runs on an abstract machine that has a correspondence to the actual machine. Typical models of computation for the abstract machine are register machines or random access machines. A typical implementation useful for static analysis consists of:

- An unlimited number of uniquely labelled registers.
- A small number of instruction prototypes to make an instruction set.
- An instruction pointer.
- A sequence of labelled instructions.
- A random access memory.
- An entry point.

The instruction set can further be divided into:

- Data (arithmetic etc.)
- Control (conditional and unconditional branching etc.)
- API Calls (operating system and library interface etc.)

4.4.3 Basic Blocks

To partition the intermediate code into basic blocks [2] we determine instructions that are leaders. Leaders are the first instruction in each basic block. An instruction is a leader when it satisfies one of the following properties:

- The first instruction in the intermediate code.
- Any instruction that is the target of a branch.
- Any instruction that follows a branch.

4.4.4 Control Flow Graph

The successors of a basic block b, succ(b), are:

- The target of the basic block's branch instruction.
- The basic block immediately following the current basic block in the instruction stream.

Thus, a control flow graph [2] is defined as the directed graph C = (B,E) such that B is the set of basic blocks, and $E = \{(u,v)|u \in B, v \in succ(u)\}$.

4.4.5 Call Graph

The successors of a procedure f, call_succ(f), are:

- The set of call targets in the procedure body.

Thus, a call graph is defined as the directed graph CallGraph = (F,E) such that F is the set of procedures, and $E = \{(u,v)|u \in F, v \in call\_succ(u)\}$.

4.5 Formal Semantics of Programming Languages

The formal semantics of programming languages aims to rigourously reason about program meaning by having a strict mathematical representation of a program's semantics. Multiple methods are available to represent program semantics and the three main techniques are:

- Operational Semantics
- Denotational Semantics
- Axiomatic Semantics

Other approaches are also possible, including algebraic semantics [3] which has been used successfully to show equivalence between code fragments of metamorphic malware.

4.5.1 Operational Semantics

Operational semantics capture the state transition that occurs when a program instruction is executed. It can be thought of as defining an interpreter for a language [4]. Operational semantics can be expressed using the following notation:

$$\frac{premise_1 \\ \ldots \\ premise_n}{(i,P) \Rightarrow P'} NAME$$

where i is the current instruction, P is the current state and P' is the next state following execution of the instruction i.

4.5.2 Denotational Semantics

Denotational semantics transform instructions to mathematical objects [4]. It can be thought of as defining a compiler for a language.

4.5.3 Axiomatic Semantics

Axiomatic semantics give an axiomatic basis for a program. Typically this is achieved by using preconditions and postconditions for instructions. These preconditions and postconditions can be analysed with logic, typically first order logic. The most common use of axiomatic semantics is to prove program correctness using Hoare logic [5] and its variants.

4.6 Theorem Proving

4.6.1 Hoare Logic

Hoare logic is a means for proving the correctness of structured programs [5]. It is based on axiomatic semantics. Hoare logic provides a deductive method for proving correctness, however loop invariants must be synthesised and this represents a significant challenge in developing program proofs.

4.6.2 Predicate Transformer Semantics

Predicate transformer semantics [6] provide a method to generate verification conditions through the weakest precondition. This is a form of axiomatic semantics and reformulates Hoare logic to provide an automated construction of first order logic formula to prove program correctness.

4.6.3 Symbolic Execution

Symbolic execution [7] is the process of executing a program using symbolic represents for variables and data. The program executes by generating constraints of the symbols for each instruction. Mixed symbolic execution [8] allows a more efficient implementation by concretely executing part of the program using native computations, and symbolically execution those variables of interest. Symbolic execution is path based execution. At every control transfer point, a decision must be made of which path to follow. The feasibility of paths and the symbolic constraints are modelled using an SMT decision procedure. The decision procedure can report if a set of constraints is feasible, or provide a counter example to prove otherwise. Symbolic execution has been applied to binaries for applications such as malware analysis [9].

4.7 Model Checking

Model checking is used to verify that a model meets the properties of a specification [10]. It achieves this by enumerating the state space of the model to verify the specification.

4.8 Data Flow Analysis

Data flow analysis tries to statically determine the behaviour of data [11]. Perfectly precise data is undecidable so data flow analysis seeks to find an approximation of the data by discovering conservative program invariants. Data flow analyses are flow-sensitive which means the ordering of instructions is taken into account. The solution of data flow problems is based on lattice and order theory. The problems are represented as monotone functions which can be approximated and computed using fixed point solutions.

4.8.1 Partially Ordered Sets

Definition 4.2 A partial order (poset) is a binary relation $\leq$ over a set P which satisfies the following conditions:

- reflexivity: $\forall x \in P : x \leq x$
- transivity: $\forall x, y, z \in P : x \leq y \wedge y \leq z \Rightarrow x \leq z$
- anti-symmetry: $\forall x, y \in P : x \leq y \wedge y \leq x \Rightarrow x = y$

Definition 4.3 Let $X \subseteq P$. $y \in P$ is an upper bound for X written as $X \leq y$ iff $\forall x \in P : x \leq y$.

Definition 4.4 Let $X \subseteq P$. $y \in P$ is a lower bound for X written as $y \leq X$ iff $\forall x \in P : y \leq x$.

4.8.2 Lattices

Definition 4.5 A lattice is a partially ordered set such that any two elements have a unique least upper bound (its supremum or join) and a unique greatest lower bound (its infimum or meet).

Definition 4.6 A complete lattice is a lattice such that all subsets have a meet and a join.

Definition 4.7 A join-semilattice is a partially ordered set such that any two elements have a join.

Definition 4.8 A meet-semilattice is a partially ordered set such that any two elements have a meet.

4.8.3 Monotone Functions and Fixed Points

Definition 4.9 A function $f : L \to L$ is monotone when $\forall x, y \in P : x \leq y \Rightarrow f(x) \leq f(y)$.

Definition 4.10 Let L be a complete lattice and let $f : L \to L$ be an order preserving function. Then the set of fixed points of f in L is also a complete lattice.

This is known as the Knaster-tarski theorem and as a consequence states the existence of a least fixed point (or greatest lower bound) in a non empty lattice given a monotone function.

4.8.4 Fixed Point Solutions to Monotone Functions

The naive algorithm to reach a fixed point for $F : L^n \rightarrow L^n$ such that $F(x_1, \ldots, x_n) = (F_1((x_1, \ldots, x_n), \ldots, F_n(x_1, \ldots, x_n))$ is

$$x = (\bot, \ldots, \bot);$$
$$do\{t = x; x = F(x); \}while(x \neq t);$$

4.8.5 Dataflow Equations

Dataflow analysis is performed by reaching a fixpoint solution in a semilattice for a system of monotone equations that describe the dataflow. Typical data flow analyses require control flow information to perform the analysis. The basic approach is to set up data flow equations to track data entering and leaving each node in the control flow graph. In a forward flow analysis, a transfer function is applied on the data entering a basic block which results in the data leaving the basic block. Merging of control flow edges is applied using a join operator. The analysis can be forwards or backwards merging successor or predecessor nodes. In some literature a meet operator is used instead of a join. This is arbitrarily dependent on whether a meet-semilattice or join-semilatice is used for analysis.

In a forward analysis using a join-semilattice, for each block b:

$$out_b = transfer\_function(in_b)$$
$$in_b = join(\{p|p \in predecessor_b\}, out_b)$$

A backwards analysis replaces in with out, and out with in. It also uses the successor blocks instead of the predecessor blocks in the join.

Typical join operators include union or intersection. Data flow analyses are usually constructed to be conservative so that precision is sacrificed to capture all possible behaviours. The analysis proceeds by iteratively computing the functions for all blocks until a fixed point is reached.

4.8.6 Dataflow Analysis Examples

Common data flow analyses include reaching definitions and live variable analysis. These analyses are use-def analyses. They resolve the problem of identifying which instructions subsequently use a variable as in the case of liveness and upwards exposed uses, or which variable definitions reach an instruction as in the case of reaching definitions. There may be more than one reaching definition of the same variable at an instruction if multiple paths lead to that instruction and the same variable is defined along those separate paths.

If an accurate control flow graph is available, then data flow analysis performs equally accurate. Data flow analyses has been heavily used in the decompilation of binaries [12]. If data flow analyses is performed interprocedurally, then the call graph must be accurately generated.

4.8.7 Reaching Definitions

The lattice for reaching definitions is the power set of definitions ordered by set inclusion. The data flow equations for reaching definitions are:

$$REACH_{OUT}[S] = GEN[S] \cup (REACH_{IN} - KILL[S])$$
$$REACH_{IN}[S] = \bigcup_{p \in pred[S]} REACH_{OUT}[p]$$
$$GEN[d : y \leftarrow f(x_1, \ldots, x_n)] = \{d\}$$
$$KILL[d : y \leftarrow f(x_1, \ldots, x_n)] = DEFS[y] - \{d\}$$

where DEFS[y] is the set of all definitions that assign to variable y. d is a unique label attached to the assigning instruction.

4.8.8 Live Variables

The lattice for live variable analysis is the power set of used variables ordered by set inclusion. The data flow equations for live variable analysis are:

$$LIVE_{IN}[S] = GEN[S] \cup (LIVE_{OUT} - KILL[S])$$
$$LIVE_{OUT}[final] = 0$$
$$LIVE_{OUT}[S] = \bigcup_{p \in succ[S]} LIVE_{IN}[p]$$
$$GEN[d : y \leftarrow f(x_1, \ldots, x_n)] = \{x_1, \ldots, x_n\}$$
$$KILL[d : y \leftarrow f(x_1, \ldots, x_n)] = DEFS[y] - \{y\}$$

4.8.9 Available Expressions

An expression is available if it is has already been computed earlier. Data flow analysis can solve the problem of identifying available expressions.

4.8.10 Very Busy Expressions

An expression is very busy if it will definitely be evaluated again before its value changes. Data flow analysis can solve the problem of identifying very busy expressions.

4.8.11 Classification of Dataflow Analyses

Data flow analyses may be categorized based on their direction and the type of join or confluence operation. A may analysis uses set union whereas a must analysis uses set intersection

	Forwards	Backwards
May	Reaching definitions	Liveness
Must	Available expressions	Very busy expressions

4.9 Abstract Interpretation

Abstract interpretation [13] is closely related to data flow analysis. Abstract interpretation concerns to the sound approximation of programs. A classic example of abstract interpretation used for pedagogical purposes is the abstract domain of signs which represents numerical variables by the possible sign they have. A variable may be positive, negative, possibly both, or zero. Abstract interpretation has been applied to, in amongst other things, malware detection.

4.9.1 Widening and Narrowing

To reach a fixed point in an ascending chain may require a long or infinite amount of time. To make this feasible, widening implements a direct short cut to the least fixed point. Widening may result in a significant over approximation, so narrowing performs the converse and leads to increasing the precision of the analysis.

4.10 Intermediate Code Optimisation

Data flow analysis is used in intermediate code optimisation. A very small set of possible optimisations are:

- Dead Store Elimination
- Constant Folding
- Copy Propagation

For example, in dead store elimination, if a variable is defined, but is not live, then the definition can be safely removed from the code.

4.11 Research Opportunities

Algebraic semantics [14] have been used to show equivalence between meta-morphic malware. However, the general approach of using formal semantics to show semantic equivalence between programs is under-utilised. We believe this presents an opportunity for researchers looking at the software similarity problem in future work. The notion of non exact matching of semantics is an area that needs investigation if we are to detect similar but not identical program copies.

References

1. Rice HG (1953) Classes of recursively enumerable sets and their decision problems. Trans Am Math Soc 74(2):358–366
2. Muchnick SS (1997) Advanced compiler design and implementation. Morgan Kaufmann, Los Altos
3. Goguen J, Malcolm G (1996) Algebraic semantics of imperative programs. MIT Press, Cambridge
4. Nielson HR, Nielson F (2007) Semantics with applications: an appetizer. Springer Verlag, NY
5. Hoare CAR (1969) An axiomatic basis for computer programming. Commun ACM 12(10):576–580. doi:10.1145/363235.363259
6. Dijkstra EW (1975) Guarded commands, nondeterminacy and formal derivation of programs. Commun ACM 18(8):453–457. doi:10.1145/360933.360975
7. King JC (1976) Symbolic execution and program testing. Commun ACM 19(7):385–394
8. Cadar C, Ganesh V, Pawlowski PM, Dill DL, Engler DR (2008) EXE: automatically generating inputs of death. ACM Trans Inf Syst Secur TISSEC (2008) 12(2):10:11–10:38. doi:10.1145/1455518.1455522
9. Brumley D, Hartwig C, Kang MG, Liang Z, Newsome J, Song D, Yin H (2007) BitScope: automatically dissecting malicious binaries. Technical report CMU-CS-07-133, school of computer science, Carnegie Mellon University
10. Clarke E (1997) Model checking. In: Foundations of software technology and theoretical computer science, pp 54–56
11. Aho AV, Sethi R, Ullman JD (1986) Compilers: principles, techniques, and tools. Addison-Wesley, Reading
12. Cifuentes C (1994) Reverse compilation techniques. Queensland University of Technology
13. Cousot P, Cousot R (1977) Abstract interpretation: a unified lattice model for static analysis of programs by construction or approximation of fixpoints. In: Sixth annual ACM SIGPLAN-SIGACT symposium on principles of programming languages, Los Angeles, California, ACM Press, pp 238–252
14. Webster M, Malcolm G (2006) Detection of metamorphic computer viruses using algebraic specification. J Comput Virol 2(3):149–161

Chapter 5
Static Analysis of Binaries

Abstract Static binary analysis is more difficult than if source code is available. In many cases, the analyses are unsound and behaviours are omitted to make problems feasible. Heuristics may be required to separate code and data in a disassembly or pointer behaviour may be weakly modelled to make statically analysing programs feasible. Nevertheless, static analysis of binaries is an important area of research with a number of practical applications including the detection of software theft and the classification and detection of malware. This chapter examines static analysis of binaries with the intent that properties and features of binary programs can be extracted to create useful birthmarks for software similarity and classification.

Keywords Disassembly · Intermediate language · Control flow reconstruction · Decompilation

5.1 Disassembly

Disassembly is the process of translating machine code to assembly language [1]. This is typically the first stage of a static analysis. Static disassembly parses the entire binary image statically without execution. In static disassembly, there are two main algorithms. In the Linear Sweep algorithm, the instructions are disassembled one instruction after another, starting from the beginning of code. The disadvantage of this method is that data introduced into instruction stream may be erroneously disassembled (Fig. 5.1).

The other main algorithm to perform disassembly is the Recursive Traversal algorithm. This algorithm decodes each instruction following the order of the control flow. This resolves the issue of embedded data, but may miss decoding instructions that are the target of indirect jumps or other situations when it is hard to resolve control flow statically (Fig. 5.2).

S. Cesare and Y. Xiang, *Software Similarity and Classification*,
SpringerBriefs in Computer Science, DOI: 10.1007/978-1-4471-2909-7_5,
© The Author(s) 2012

```
disassemble_program(program)
{
  address = disassemble_linear_sweep(
    start(program), end(program))
}

disassemble_linear_sweep(start, end) {
  address = start
  while (address < end) {
    instruction = Disassemble(program, address)
    if (error) {
      address += 1;
    } else {
      disassembly[address] = instruction;
      address += length(instruction);
    }
  }
}
```

Fig. 5.1 Linear sweep disassembly

```
disassemble_program(program) {
  disassemble(entry_point(program))
}
disassemble_recursive_traversal(address) {
  while (has_address(program, address)) {
    if (disassembly[address] not null)
     return
    instruction = Disassemble(program, address)
    if (error)
      return
    disassembly[address] = instruction
    if (is_return_instruction(instruction))
      return
    if (is_transfer_instruction(instruction))
      disassemble(transfer_target(instruction);
    address += length(instruction);
  }
}
```

Fig. 5.2 Recursive traversal disassembly

Speculative Disassembly attempts to remedy the problems of the Recursive Traversal algorithm problem by first performing the Recursive Traversal, and then performing a Linear Sweep in regions that are not decoded (Fig. 5.3).

Disassembly results in the following data.

$$disassembly = \{address, opcode, operand_1, \ldots, operand_n\}$$

5.2 Intermediate Code Generation

A simple approach to transforming assembly into an intermediate language is to translate each instruction without maintaining intermediate state. This approach has been used successfully in the Reverse Engineering Intermediate Language

```
disassemble_speculative(program) {
  disassemble_recursive_traversal(entry_point(program))
  for all intervals in
    [start(program), end(program)] and not in disassembly
  {
    disassemble_linear_sweep(
      start(interval), end(interval))
  }
}
```

Fig. 5.3 Speculative disassembly

```
disassemble_procedure(address) {
  while (has_address(program, address)) {
    if (disassembly[address] not null)
      return
    instruction = Disassemble(program, address)
    if (error)
      return
    disassembly[address] = instruction
    if (is_return_instruction(instruction))
      return
    if (is_transfer_instruction(instruction)
        and not is_call_instruction(instruction))
      disassemble_procedure(transfer_target(instruction);
    address += length(instruction);
  }
}
```

Fig. 5.4 Procedure disassembly

(REIL) [2]. Other popular intermediate languages are Vex as used in the Valgrind binary instrumentation framework [3] and Vine as used in the BitBlaze project [4]. An example to translate native assembly into three address code is shown below.

$$native\_assembly\_instruction \rightarrow (TAC_1, \ldots TAC_n)$$

5.3 Procedure Identification

An important stage in reconstruction the control flow of an executable is identifying procedures. There are roughly four approaches that can be employed (Fig. 5.4).

- Using object file format information (e.g., symbols and exports)
- Using static targets of call site $F = \{f | (address, call\_direct, f) \in disassembly\}$
- Using idioms to identify procedure prologues
- Using static analysis and data flow analysis to reconstruct indirect call targets

The main hindrance to generating accurate representations is when a program uses indirect branches and procedure calls. The analysis of indirect targets requires data flow analysis. A number of approaches have been employed [5–7]. Using idioms to identify procedures requires string matching algorithms to identify common byte sequences.

5.4 Procedure Disassembly

Procedures consist of a body of instructions which must be recovered from the disassembly. The algorithm is a very slight variation of the recursive traversal disassembly algorithm. The difference is that inter procedural control flow is not traversed.

5.5 Control Flow Analysis, Deobfuscation and Reconstruction

Control flow analysis is more difficult on binaries because of the difficultly in separating code and data. Likewise, the presence of indirect branch and call targets in assembly language makes precisely determining the static control flow undecidable.

The simplest approach is to ignore indirect targets completely. The edges of the graphs representing the call graph control flow can be constructed by connecting the call site to the static call target. For control flow graphs the approach is similarly applied to branch targets.

Control flow may also be obfuscated. An opaque predicate [8] is a predicate that always evaluates to the same result. An opaque predicate is constructed so that it is difficult for an analyst or automated analysis to know the predicate result. Opaque predicates can be used to insert superfluous branching in a binary's control flow. They can also be used to assign variables values which are hard to determine statically. The use of opaque predicates is primarily for code obfuscation, and to prevent understanding by an analyst or automated static analysis.

The presence of opaque predicates in a control flow graph reduces the accuracy of the graph because of misleading branch targets. In [9] it was proposed to use the program analysis technique of abstract interpretation to detect specific classes of opaque predicate algorithms.

5.6 Pointer Analysis

Pointer and alias analysis tries to determine the variables that a pointer may point to. In assembly this problem is difficult. A conservative approach to alias analysis of assembly using datalog constraints was proposed in [10], however, this work was to introduce formal rigour and is not practical to deploy. Value-Set Analysis [11] has been proposed as an alias analysis, suitable for binary programs and assembly language. Value-Set Analysis has been used in malware detection [12] and the automated static unpacking of malware [13].

5.7 Decompilation of Binaries

Decompilation [14] is the process of recovering source code from executable binaries. In general, decompilation can be seen as a form of static analysis of a binary that recovers additional information from its intermediate representation. Research connecting the type of static analysis a compiler performs to the requirements of a decompiler was proposed in [14, 15].

5.7.1 Condition Code Elimination

In Instruction Set Architectures such as x86, many arithmetical instructions modify a status flag or condition code. For example, determining if two variables are equal is divided into two computations. An arithmetic instruction over the two variables that sets a condition code, and then a branch based on the resulting condition code. Decompilation requires these two computations be reduced to one conditional test.

An approach to solve this is by maintaining a reaching definition of the various conditions code set by each arithmetic instruction. At the point of a conditional branch based on the condition code, the reaching definitions are combined into a single condition.

5.7.2 Stack Variable Reconstruction

Stack variable reconstruction transforms variables allocated on the stack into native variables in the intermediate representation. The stack can be accessed in two main ways. The first method is by referencing variables relative to the top of the stack, or stack pointer. The second method accesses the stack relative to the frame pointer. The frame pointer is unique for each procedure or activation record. It points to the top of the stack as set on function entry. During procedure execution the stack pointer may change, but the frame pointer remains constant. This simplifies access to variables on the stack and is often used in debug builds of application. It is clear that for a decompiler to be effective, it must handle both methods of accessing the stack. Both frame and stack based addressing may be intermixed in real life applications.

Another complication to using the stack pointer is that callees may or may not change the stack pointer. It is the responsibility of the caller to push arguments onto the stack, but the callee may or may not unwind these arguments based on the calling convention being used.

One approach [16] to reconstruct stack based variables takes advantage of the fact that in compiled programs, the position of the stack pointer in each basic block remains constant. The stack pointer can be modified within a basic block when calls are made or values or pushed and popped on or from the stack. Using this information, a set of constraints over the control flow graph can describe the stack pointer. Solving the constraints identifies the relative position of the stack pointer at the entry and exit of each basic block. Frame pointer relative addressing uses fixed offsets from the top of the stack at the beginning of the procedure, and knowing the position of the stack pointer at each basic block enables knowing exactly which memory location on the stack is being referenced. This enables a unified approach to modelling stack and frame based addressing.

Pointers and arrays complicate the process of stack variable reconstruction. In these cases, the stack variable may only be referencing the beginning of an array or pointing to the beginning of the object. Heuristics must be used to estimate the size of the object. An approach to estimate this is by looking at the size of the stack frame or looking at the next adjacent stack reference to predict a bounds on the object in question.

5.7.3 Preserved Register Detection

A typical problem that arises is determining if the register is modified in the life time of a procedure. If the register is used in procedure, but maintains its original value once returning from the procedure's callsite then the register is preserved. The process of preserving a register is to copy the register into a temporary variable and then restore it before leaving the function. Detecting preserved registers is important in the process of identifying which registers are arguments or return values from a procedure.

Data flow analysis and a suitable intermediate representation can help solve the preserved register problem. If we ignore calls within a procedure, we can identify a preserved register by the fact that the reaching definitions for that register at each function exit, is the value of a copy of the register on function entry. To determine where the value is copied on entry to the function we can use a liveness analysis to identify where the register is used and check that instruction for a copy instruction.

This process of identifying preserved registers requires that local variable reconstruction be performed. The reason is that the temporary variable used to save a copy of the preserved register is typically represented by a local variable.

5.7.4 Procedure Parameter Reconstruction

The parameters to procedures may be passed on the stack, or passed via registers. The return values are typically passed by registers. The exact semantics are defined

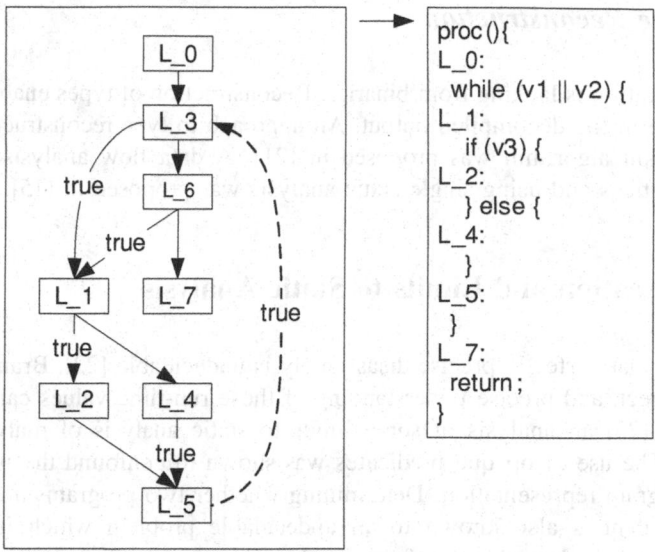

Fig. 5.5 A control flow graph and its linearized form

the calling convention on a particular procedure. The arguments used by a procedure can be determined by the procedure accessing variables outside the current stack frame. Once the arguments are known, at call sites, the stack is statically unwound to the required depth to retrieve them.

Registers may also be passed as arguments. Ignoring calls, arguments are registers that are live on procedure entry that aren't preserved. To take into account calls, the analysis is performed on inner calls first as defined by their depth first order in the call graph. Recursive calls require further analysis.

5.7.5 Reconstruction of Structured Control Flow

A standard technique in decompilation is transforming a control flow graph into higher level structured control flow [14, 17, 18]. This is the process of structuring. Identifying conditions, loops, and parts of the control flow graph that cannot be structured is required. Conditions may be compound conditional statements involving conjunction and disjunction. The higher the quality of structuring means the less the number of gotos in the generated code. Some graphs cannot be structured and the reducibility of the graph identifies these cases.

Structuring of control flow graphs was proposed in [19, 20] to generate string signatures that were later used to identify malware variants (Fig. 5.5).

5.7.6 Type Reconstruction

Type information is lacking from binaries. Reconstruction of types enables higher quality code in the decompiled output. An approach to type reconstruction using the unification algorithm was proposed in [21]. A data flow analysis approach based on lattices and using single static analysis was proposed in [15].

5.8 Obfuscation and Limits to Static Analysis

It is known that perfectly precise disassembly is undecidable [22]. Branch targets can be indirect, and precise understanding of those run-time values can be problematic. In [23] an analysis of some limits to static analysis of malware were identified. The use of opaque predicates was shown to confound the problem of precise program representation. Determining whether two programs are semantically equivalent is also known to an undecidable problem which is why for example malware detection is often based on heuristic and unsound solutions. Likewise, perfect decompilation, for all possible binaries, is undecidable. If the binary does not originate from high level source then it is unlikely decompilation will give meaningful results.

5.9 Research Opportunities

Decompilation presents potential research opportunities when combined with other techniques such as static analysis or malware classification. Very little research has been performed on decompilation-based applications. The main application of decompilation thus far has been source code recovery. However, the high level information it recovers makes it a suitable abstraction for useful software features.

References

1. Kruegel C, Robertson W, Valeur F, Vigna G (2004) Static disassembly of obfuscated binaries. In: USENIX security symposium, p 18
2. Dullien T, Porst S (2009) REIL: a platform-independent intermediate representation of disassembled code for static code analysis. In: CanSecWest applied security conference, 2009
3. Nethercote N, Seward J (2003) Valgrind a program supervision framework. Electron Notes Theor Comput Sci 89(2):44–66
4. Song D, Brumley D, Yin H, Caballero J, Jager I, Kang M, Liang Z, Newsome J, Poosankam P, Saxena P (2008) BitBlaze: a new approach to computer security via binary analysis. Information systems security, pp 1–25
5. Kästner D, Stephan W (2002) Generic control flow reconstruction from assembly code. SIGPLAN Not 37(7):46–55. doi:http://doi.acm.org/10.1145/566225.513839

6. Theiling H (2000) Extracting safe and precise control flow from binaries. Paper presented at the proceedings of the 7th international conference on real-time systems and applications

7. Johannes K, Florian Z, Helmut V (2009) An abstract interpretation-based framework for control flow reconstruction from binaries. Paper presented at the proceedings of the 10th international conference on verification, model checking, and abstract interpretation, Savannah

8. Cullen L, Saumya D (2003) Obfuscation of executable code to improve resistance to static disassembly. Paper presented at the proceedings of the 10th ACM conference on computer and communications security, Washington

9. Dalla Preda M, Madou M, De Bosschere K, Giacobazzi R (2006) Opaque predicates detection by abstract interpretation. Algebraic methodology and software technology, pp 81–95

10. Brumley D, Newsome J (2006) Alias analysis for assembly. Technical Report CMU-CS-06-180, Carnegie Mellon University School of Computer Science, 2006

11. Balakrishnan G, Reps T, Melski D, Teitelbaum T (2007) Wysinwyx: What you see is not what you execute. Verified software: theories, tools, experiments, pp 202–213

12. Leder F, Steinbock B, Martini P (2009) Classification and detection of metamorphic malware using value set analysis. In: Proceedings of 4th international conference on malicious and unwanted software (Malware 2009), Montreal, 2009

13. Debray KCS, Townsend TKG (2009) Automatic Static Unpacking of Malware Binaries. Paper presented at the working conference on reverse engineering—WCRE

14. Cifuentes C (1994) Reverse compilation techniques. Queensland University of Technology

15. Van Emmerik MJ (2007) Static single assignment for decompilation. The University of Queensland

16. Hex-Rays S (2008) IDA Pro Disassembler

17. Moretti E, Chanteperdrix G, Osorio A (2001) New algorithms for control-flow graph structuring. Paper presented at the software maintenance and reengineering

18. Wei T, Mao J, Zou W, Chen Y (2007) Structuring 2-way branches in binary executables. Paper presented at the international computer software and applications conference

19. Cesare S, Xiang Y (2010) Classification of malware using structured control flow. In: 8th Australasian symposium on parallel and distributed computing (AusPDC 2010)

20. Cesare S, Xiang Y (2010) A fast flowgraph based classification system for packed and polymorphic Malware on the Endhost. In: IEEE 24th international conference on advanced information networking and application (AINA)

21. Mycroft A (1999) Type-based decompilation. Lecture notes in computer science, vol 1576. Springer, Heidelberg, pp 208–223

22. Horspool RN, Marovac N (1979) An approach to the problem of detranslation of computer programs. Comput J 23(3):223–229

23. Moser A, Kruegel C, Kirda E (2007) Limits of static analysis for malware detection. In: Annual computer security applications conference (ACSAC), 2007

Chapter 6
Dynamic Analysis

Abstract In the previous chapters we have examined static extraction of program features for the purpose of birthmark construction. Dynamic analysis is examined in this chapter. It is an alternative approach to static analysis that can be used for birthmark construction. Dynamic analysis concerns itself with analysing a running program. The program being run is typically isolated in an environment which allows its behaviour to be inspected. Typical behaviours that are extracted are the API call sequence. Instruction sequences, basic block sequences and control flow are amongst other behaviours that can also be identified.

Keywords Dynamic analysis · Hooking · Dynamic binary instrumentation · Virtualization · Application level emulation · Whole system emulation

6.1 Relationship to Static Analysis

There are roughly two approaches to extract program features from software. In the static approach, the software is never executed and the features are extracted from a static view of the program. In dynamic analysis the software is executed, possibly in a virtual machine, and its run-time behaviour examined. The run-time behaviours exhibit the properties or features being extracted.

Static analysis is effective because it is able to examine to represent the set of all possible execution paths by approximating program behaviour. This is important because behaviours of specific programs may be hard to trigger dynamically. It is often difficult to trigger corner cases in programs and as a result a number of dynamic analysis testing methodologies exist to address this such as the use of analysing code coverage during execution. In the case of malicious code, malware authors actively change the behaviour of the code when under analysis.

S. Cesare and Y. Xiang, *Software Similarity and Classification*,
SpringerBriefs in Computer Science, DOI: 10.1007/978-1-4471-2909-7_6,
© The Author(s) 2012

The main advantage of dynamic analysis is that the semantics of the program are exhibited, and obfuscations applied to the program have less effect on these exhibited semantics. Attempting to identify run-time behaviour properties for multiple paths of execution has been researched [1]. It is still a new area, but using symbolic execution to trigger different behaviours has had some success. The results of exploring these multiple paths can be accumulated into a final report to infer the intent or potential behaviour of a piece of software.

6.2 Environments

Dynamic analysis requires an environment in which to run and isolate the program being analysed. The environment in which to run a program can be categorized in the following list:

- Hooking
- Dynamic Binary Instrumentation
- Virtualization
- Application Level Emulation
- Whole System Emulation

6.3 Debugging

An operating system typically provides an API to debug processes. Debugging can allow for operations including single stepping through execution an instruction at a time, or setting a breakpoint at a particular code address. Debugging can be useful to monitor non malicious programs, however, most malware today implements anti-debugging functionality which can detect the presence of a debugger.

6.4 Hooking

Hooking is the process of intercepting API calls allowing for possible instrumentation. Hooks can be placed in user space or kernel space. Hooking is commonly used by commercial Antivirus software to monitor process behaviour and detect possible misuse. Detours [2] is an implementation of hooking for the Windows operating system. The basic mode of operation is to overwrite the function in memory with a trampoline to the intercept handling code. The intercept handling code performs any instrumentation or monitoring as necessary then restores control back to the original function. Another method of hooking is overwriting dispatch tables such as system call tables or import addresses. It is also possible in Linux to natively intercept API calls to dynamic libraries by preloading another library. Malware today often can detect the presence of hooking by implementing checksums over their executable code.

6.5 Dynamic Binary Instrumentation

Dynamic binary instrumentation is an approach that instruments native code on the fly. The binary being executed is controlled from a dispatcher which analyses the code, instruments it, and then rewrites it for execution. Some examples of dynamic binary instrumentation include PIN [3], DynamoRIO [4], and Valgrind [5]. Dynamic binary instrumentation based on PIN has been used for malware unpacking and analysis in [6, 7].

6.6 Virtualization

Virtualization is a technique that supports native execution of a guest operating system by exploiting separation and isolation mechanisms implemented by the native hardware architecture or software. A number of methods are available to implement virtualization including paravirtualization which must be supported by both the host and the guest operating systems. The most important type of virtualization for providing an environment to perform feature extractions is hardware assisted virtualization. In the x86 architecture, hardware assisted virtualization was not always supported and detection of the virtualized environment was implemented by many strains of malware [6]. Hardware assisted virtualization has been used for malware analysis [8]. This type of analysis is harder to detect but attacks still exist to detect virtualization from a guest [9]. For example, it is known that memory caching between guests and hosts are different in the virtualized environment. However, as virtualization becomes a standard tool on the desktop, malware authors might no longer be able to associate virtualization with threat analysis.

6.7 Application Level Emulation

Application level emulation emulates the operating system and instruction set architecture for specific applications. This approach has been predominantly employed in Antivirus systems to perform real-time analysis of malware and automated unpacking [10]. Its main disadvantage is its inability to faithfully emulate the desired system which makes it susceptible to detection as has been the case with modern malware.

The typical features emulated in an application level emulator on the x86 Windows platform for the purposes of malware detection include:

- Instruction Set Architecture (ISA).
- Virtual Memory.
- Windows API emulation.
- Linking and Loading.
- Thread and Process Management.
- OS Specific Structures.

The instruction set architecture (ISA) must be faithfully emulated. In practice, most deployed emulators only simulate part of the complete x86 ISA. Malware authors have responded by using uncommon instructions such as those associated with MMX and FPU to detect and thwart the emulation process.

Virtual memory must be emulated. 32-bit x86 employs a segmented memory architecture. In Windows the segment registers are utilised to reference thread specific data. This data is additionally used by Windows Structured Exception Handling (SEH). SEH is used to gracefully handle abnormal conditions such as division by zero and is routinely used by packers and malware to obfuscate control flow.

The Windows API is the official system call interface provided by Windows. There are too many Windows API functions to full emulate in a typical environment so only the most common APIs are implemented. This also presents a method for malware to detect and thwart an emulator using uncommon API calls.

Linking and loading must be implemented by an emulator. Program loading entails allocating the appropriate virtual memory, loading the program text, data and dynamic libraries. Relocations must be performed and run-time linking performed.

Threads and process management must be performed. Malware can sometimes try to detect and thwart a debugger or emulator by being multi-process or multi-threaded.

OS specific structures must also be simulated. Windows has a number of these including the Process Environment Block, the Thread Environment Block and the Loader Module. These structures are visible to applications and can be used by malware.

6.8 Whole System Emulation

A whole system emulator emulates the hardware of a PC. This allows an operating system to be installed as a guest. There are roughly two approaches to implement a whole system emulator or any emulator in general:

- Interpretation
- Dynamic Binary Instrumentation

An example of whole system emulators includes QEMU [11] which is based on dynamic binary translation. Bochs is another whole system emulator that uses interpretation instead of dynamic binary translation. Bochs has been used for malware unpacking and analysis [12]. Interpretation is slower than dynamic binary translation which makes QEMU a popular choice.

Interpretation works by implementing a fetch, decode and execute loop inside the emulator. Dynamic binary translation translates sequences of code from the guest into native code on the host. It can perform optimisations on these blocks of code which improves efficiency. The blocks are also cached reducing the costs of translation. In general, dynamic binary translation offers significant performance improvements over an interpretation based emulator.

It is possible to modify a whole system emulator to monitor or instrument guest execution [13]. The BitBlaze project [14] is a project for binary analysis that makes heavy use of whole system emulation to perform tasks including malware analysis. Whole system emulation is effective for behavioural analysis of code but attacks exist to detect its presence from the guest [9].

References

1. Brumley D, Hartwig C, Kang MG, Liang Z, Newsome J, Song D, Yin H (2007) BitScope: automatically dissecting malicious binaries. Technical report CMU-CS-07-133, School of Computer Science, Carnegie Mellon University
2. Hunt G, Brubacher D (1999) Detours: binary interception of win32 functions. Paper presented at the proceedings of the 3rd conference on USENIX Windows NT symposium, vol 3. Seattle, Washington
3. Luk CK, Cohn R, Muth R, Patil H, Klauser A, Lowney G, Wallace S, Reddi VJ, Hazelwood K (2005) Pin: building customized program analysis tools with dynamic instrumentation. Paper presented at the proceedings of the 2005 ACM SIGPLAN conference on programming language design and implementation
4. Bala V, Duesterwald E, Banerjia S (2000) Dynamo: a transparent dynamic optimization system. Paper presented at the proceedings of the ACM SIGPLAN 2000 conference on programming language design and implementation
5. Nethercote N, Seward J (2003) Valgrind a program supervision framework. Electron Notes Theor Comput Sci 89(2):44–66
6. Guizani W, Marion JY, Reynaud-Plantey D (2009) Server-side dynamic code analysis. In: Malicious and unwanted software (MALWARE), 2009 4th international conference on, 2009, pp 55–62
7. Quist D (2007) Valsmith covert debugging circumventing software armoring techniques. In: Black hat briefings USA
8. Dinaburg A, Royal P, Sharif M, Lee W Ether (2008) Malware analysis via hardware virtualization extensions. In: Proceedings of the 15th ACM conference on computer and communications security 2008. ACM, New York, USA, pp 51–62
9. Raffetseder T, Kruegel C, Kirda E (2007) Detecting system emulators. In: Lecture notes in computer science, vol 4779, p 1
10. Cesare S, Xiang Y (2010) Classification of malware using structured control flow. In: 8th Australasian symposium on parallel and distributed computing (AusPDC 2010
11. Bellard F (2005) QEMU, a fast and portable dynamic translator. In: USENIX annual technical conference 2005, pp 41–46
12. Boehne L (2008) Pandora's bochs: automatic unpacking of malware. University of Mannheim

13. Bayer U, Kruegel C, Kirda E (2006) TTAnalyze: a tool for analyzing malware. In: European Institute for Computer Antivirus Research (EICAR), 2006
14. Song D, Brumley D, Yin H, Caballero J, Jager I, Kang M, Liang Z, Newsome J, Poosankam P, Saxena P (2008) BitBlaze: a new approach to computer security via binary analysis. In: Information systems security

Chapter 7
Feature Extraction

Abstract In the previous chapters we have examined static and dynamic methods of program analysis. These features must be translated into mathematical representations and birthmarks to be useful. Furthermore, mathematical representations may be embedded in other mathematical types to make birthmarks more amenable to similarity comparisons and for use in classification algorithms. Another approach is to represent features using kernels. This allows for the use of classification algorithms including the support vector machine for complex data types. This chapter examines the mathematical representations that we use to describe program features.

Keywords Program feature processing · Strings · Vectors · Sets · Sets of vectors · Trees · Graphs · Embeddings · Kernels

7.1 Processing Program Features

Program features are the basis of software similarity and classification, but must be transformed or into a meaningful representation that allows for similarity comparisons and indexing. Different representations are possible ranging from highly efficient but least expressive, to highly expressive but least efficient. For example, representing birthmarks as vectors allows for very efficient comparisons, but tends to lose structural information that is present in graph based representations.

Combining features into a unified form may result in the establishment of software metrics. Attribute counting is one approach. Attributes that can be tallied might include the number of specific keywords, the number of conditionals, the number of loops and so forth. The final metric is the set of counted attributes. Processing might be done on these counted attributes to result in other measures.

S. Cesare and Y. Xiang, *Software Similarity and Classification*,
SpringerBriefs in Computer Science, DOI: 10.1007/978-1-4471-2909-7_7,
© The Author(s) 2012

The Halstead complexity measures [1] are a set of software metrics that uses attribute counting at its core to give a measure on a programs complexity. Its initial use was for the purpose of software maintenance metrics but it has also been applied to software similarity.

Another approach to combine the expressiveness of complex objects, such as graphs, is to transform or embed one representation into another. For example, a graph can be transformed into a vector based representation. Information is lost, but in many cases this is still useful as a birthmark.

7.2 Strings

A string describes a sequence of tokens or characters. An example of a string could be a sequence of instruction opcodes making up a program path.

Definition 7.1 Let $\sum$ be an alphabet of symbols. Let s be a string over the alphabet where $s \in \sum^*$.

7.3 Vectors

Vectors are one of the simplest representations and are efficient to work with. A vector is an ordered list or tuple of a fixed number of elements or dimensions. A feature vector describes the frequency of particular features occurring. If the number of features is very large then dimensionality reduction can be used to filter unimportant features, or combine features together such as when using Principle Component Analysis (PCA).

Examples of using vectors include describing features based on the occurrence of a specific n characters or n-grams.

7.4 Sets

A set is a collection of unique objects. A set of features is sometimes a useful representation. It ignores ordering of those features. An example use of sets is to describe the set of API calls a program makes.

7.5 Sets of Vectors

A set of vectors may sometimes be useful. If we consider that a procedure can be represented as a vector, then the set of procedures can be represented as a set of vectors.

7.6 Trees

Trees capture the structure of data, but are not as general as graphs. A tree is a connected undirected graph without cycles. Abstract syntax trees and parse trees are naturally represented by trees. Structured control flow can also be represented by trees. Trees can have a defined ordering of child nodes or be unordered.

7.7 Graphs

Graphs model structure in the data. Many program features are naturally represented as graphs include control flow graphs, call graphs, and dependency graphs.

Definition 7.2 A graph is $g = (V, E)$ where V is a set of vertices. $E = \{(u, v) \mid u, v \in V\} \subseteq V \times V$

Definition 7.3 A labelled graph $g = (V, \alpha, \beta)$ where V is a set of vertices $\alpha : V \to L$ is the node labelling function, and $\beta : V \times V \to L$ is the edge labelling function.

7.8 Embeddings

Strings may be embedded in vectors. To reduce the string problem into an n-gram vector problem, a string may be divided into n-grams where the specific n-grams represent features.

Definition 7.4 Given a set of strings L, and a set of vectors V there is a function f such that $f : L \to V$

Strings may be embedded in sets. To reduce the string problem into a set problem, a string may be divided into n-grams or shingles where the unique n-grams represent set elements.

Definition 7.5 Given a set of strings L, and a set of sets S there is a function f such that $f : L \to S$

Trees may be embedded in vectors. A tree may be decomposed into fixed sized subtrees. These subtrees can represent features in a feature vector.

Definition 7.6 Given a set of trees T, and a set of vectors V there is a function f such that $f : T \to V$

Trees may be embedded in sets. Similar to a tree to vector problem, decomposing the tree into unique features can be represented by sets.

Definition 7.7 Given a set of trees T, and a set of sets S there is a function f such that $f : T \to S$

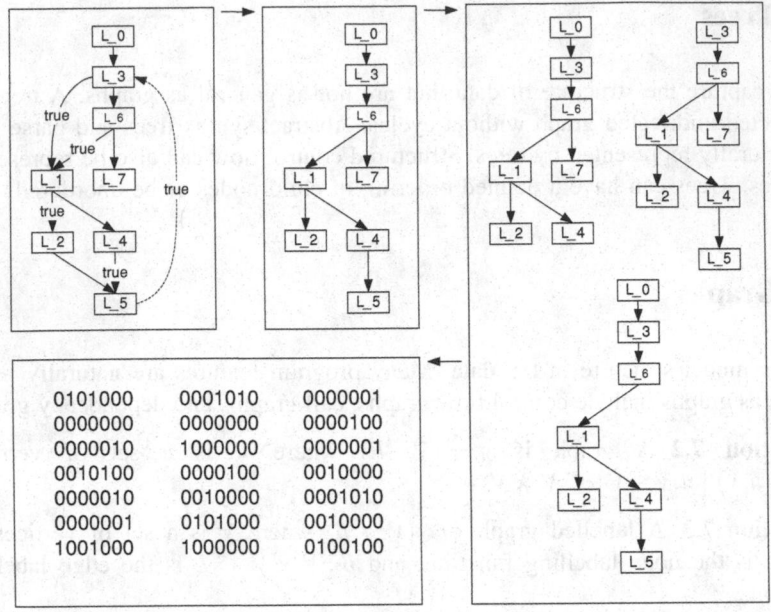

Fig. 7.1 The k-subgraph feature for a graph embedding in a vector

A graph may be embedded in a vector. A graph can be decomposed into fixed sized k-subgraphs. One approach is to construct a spanning tree and then extract the subgraphs. These subgraphs can be canonized into strings and used to represent features in a feature vector. Another approach to embedding a set of control flow graphs into a vector is by embedding the graphs into strings using decompilation and then embedding the strings into vectors using k-grams [2] (Fig. 7.1).

Definition 7.8 Given a set of graphs G, and a set of vectors V there is a function f such that $f : G \rightarrow V$

A graph may be embedded in a set. Transforming a graph into a set is analogous to a graph to vector problem.

Definition 7.9 Given a set of graphs G, and a set of sets S there is a function f such that $f : G \rightarrow S$

A graph may be embedded in a tree. A graph can be represented by tree by constructing a spanning tree.

Definition 7.10 Given a set of graphs G, and a set of trees T there is a function f such that $f : G \rightarrow T$

7.9 Kernels

Kernels are most used in kernel based statistical machine learning classifiers. A kernel function operates in feature space which is typically of much higher dimensionality. A string kernel based on the subsequences in the string known as a subsequence kernels was proposed in [3]. A kernel for sets of features was proposed in [4]. A kernel for vector sets was proposed in [5]. A kernel for trees was proposed in [6]. A kernel based on random walks in a graph was proposed in [7]. Subtree kernels have been proposed. A kernel based the set of all paths in a graph has also been proposed. A kernel based on the shortest paths in a graph was proposed in [8].

7.10 Research Opportunities

Embeddings and kernels present a significant opportunity for researchers. Embeddings have been investigated somewhat, but a comprehensive treatment of different embeddings for different structures has not been performed in the context of software similarity. Kernel methods are effectively unused in software similarity and this presents many opportunities for researchers to apply kernel methods to so the software similarity and classification problem. Graph kernels could be used to perform software classification in applications such as malware classification.

References

1. Halstead MH (1977) Elements of software science (operating and programming systems series). Elsevier Science Inc, NY
2. Cesare S, Xiang Y (2011) Malware variant detection using similarity search over sets of control flow graphs. In: IEEE Trustcom
3. Lodhi H, Saunders C, Shawe-Taylor J, Cristianini N, Watkins C (2002) Text classification using string kernels. J Mach Learn Res 2:419–444
4. Grauman K, Darrell T (2007) The pyramid match kernel: efficient learning with sets of features. J Mach Learn Res 8:725–760
5. Kondor R, Jebara T (2003) A kernel between sets of vectors. In: Proceedings of ICML'2003, vol 1, p 361
6. Collins M, Duffy N (2002) Convolution kernels for natural language. Adv Neural Inf Process Syst 1:625–632
7. Kashima H, Inokuchi A (2002) Kernels for graph classification, p 25
8. Borgwardt KM, Kriegel HP (2005) Shortest-path kernels on graphs. In: Data mining

Chapter 8
Software Birthmark Similarity

Abstract Comparing birthmarks is necessary to identify similarities between software. If two birthmarks are similar, then the software is similar. Birthmarks may be compared to show similarity, or an alternative to showing similarity is to show dissimilarity or distance. Similarity measures and metrics exist for the different types of data such as strings, vectors, trees, graphs, etc. This chapter examines the different similarity measures and metrics for the different classes of birthmarks.

Keywords Birthmark similarity · Distance metrics · String similarity · Vector similarity · Set similarity · Set of vectors similarity · Tree similarity · Graph similarity

8.1 Distance Metrics

Definition 8.1 A metric on a set X is a function (known as the distance function or distance):

$$d : X \times D \to \mathbb{N}$$

For all x, y, z in X, this function is required to satisfy the following conditions:

1. $d(x, y) \geq 0$
2. $d(x, y) = 0$ *iff* $x = y$
3. $d(x, y) = d(y, x)$
4. $d(x, z) \leq d(x, y) + d(y, z)$ *(triangle inequality)*

S. Cesare and Y. Xiang, *Software Similarity and Classification,*
SpringerBriefs in Computer Science, DOI: 10.1007/978-1-4471-2909-7_8,
© The Author(s) 2012

If the distance function has the properties of a distance metric then indexing and searching a database can be performed more efficiently. Therefore, it is beneficial to compare software using distance functions that are metric. Examples of metric access methods are in [1–3].

8.2 String Similarity

Strings can be compared using string metrics. The Levenshtein distance between two strings defines the number of edit operations that must be performed to transform one string to the other. An edit operation includes character insertion, deletion, and substitution. Other string metrics include the Smith-Waterman algorithm which is used to perform local string alignment, or using the longest common subsequence. Optimal solutions to edit distance and alignments are normally O(n.m) where n and m are the lengths of each respective string. The solutions are typically implemented using dynamic programming. The Levenshtein distance, Smith-Waterman distance and Normalized Compression Distance are all metric.

8.2.1 Levenshtein Distance

Definition 8.2 For two strings s and t, the Levenshtein distance is measured as follows:

$$D(i,0) = 0 \quad 0 \leq i \leq len(s)$$

$$D(0,j) = 0 \quad 0 \leq j \leq len(t)$$

$$D(i,j) = \min \begin{cases} D(i-1,j-1) + d(si,tj), & substitution \\ D(i-1,j) + 1, & insertion \\ D(i,j-1) + 1 & deletion \end{cases}$$

$d(i,j)$ is a function whereby $d(c,d) = 0$ if $c = d$, 1 else.

The Levenshtein distance is metric.

Definition 8.3 A method of normalizing the edit distance to give a similarity in [0,1] is:

$$sim(s,t) = 1 - \frac{ed(s,t)}{\max(len(s), len(t))}$$

8.2.2 Smith-Waterman Algorithm

Definition 8.4 For two strings s and t, the Smith-Waterman similarity score is measured as follows:

$$D(i,0) = 0 \quad 0 \leq i \leq len(s)$$

$$D(0,j) = 0 \quad 0 \leq j \leq len(t)$$

If $a_i = b_j w(a_i, b_j) = w(match)$ or $a_i \neq b_j w(a_i, b_j) = w(mismatch)$

$$D(i,j) = \max \begin{cases} 0 \\ H(i-1,j-1) + w(ai,bj) & match/mismatch \\ H(i-1,j) + w(ai,-) & deletion \\ H(i,j-1) + w(-,bj) & insertion \end{cases}$$

The Smith-Waterman algorithm when constructed as a distance instead of a similarity is known to be metric. The similarity algorithm is known as an optimal local string alignment.

8.2.3 Longest Common Subsequence (LCS)

Definition 8.5 For two strings X and Y, the *LCS* is found as follows:

$LCS(Xi, Yi) =$

$$\begin{cases} 0 & if\ i = 0\ or\ j = 0 \\ (LCS(Xi-1, Yj-1), xi) & if\ xi = yj \\ longest(LCS(Xi, Yj-1), LCS(Xi-1, Yj)) & if\ xi \neq yj \end{cases}$$

The similarity between two strings X and Y is defined as $|LCS(X, Y)|$.

8.2.4 Normalized Compression Distance

Definition 8.6 For two strings x and y where $C(x)$ is the length of a compressed x, the normalized compression distance (*NCD*) [4] is:

$$NCD(x,y) = \frac{C(x,y) - \min(C(x), C(y))}{\max(C(x), C(y))}$$

The NCD is metric.

8.3 Vector Similarity

Vector distance can be performed using metrics such as the Euclidean distance or Manhattan distance. Non metric similarity measures can include the cosine similarity which is often used in text mining.

8.3.1 Euclidean Distance

Definition 8.7 The Euclidean distance between vectors p and q is:

$$d(p,q) = \sqrt{\sum_{i=1}^{n} (q_i - p_i)^2}$$

The Euclidean distance is metric.

8.3.2 Manhattan Distance

Definition 8.8 The Manhattan distance between vectors p and q is:

$$d(p,q) = \sum_{i=1}^{n} |q_i - p_i|$$

The Manhattan distance is metric.

8.3.3 Cosine Similarity

Definition 8.9 The cosine similarity between vectors A and B is:

$$similarity = \cos(\varphi) = \frac{A \cdot B}{\|A\|\|B\|}$$

The cosine similarity is not metric.

8.4 Set Similarity

Two sets can be compared using a variety of measures. The Dice coefficient and Jaccard Index are two such measures. The Jaccard Index is not metric, but its parallel the Jaccard Distance is, which allows for efficient indexing and searching. Containment and the Tversky index are examples of asymmetric similarity measures. Because they are asymmetric, they do not qualify as metric distance functions.

8.4.1 Dice Coefficient

Definition 8.10 The Dice coefficient between sets A and B is:

$$s = \frac{2|A \cap B|}{|A| + |B|}$$

The Dice coefficient is not metric.

8.4.2 Jaccard Index

Definition 8.11 The Jaccard Index between sets A and B is:

$$J(A, B) = \frac{|A \cap B|}{|A \cup B|}$$

The Jaccard Index is not metric, however, the Jaccard distance is.

8.4.3 Jaccard Distance

Definition 8.12 The Jaccard distance between sets A and B is:

$$J_d(A, B) = 1 - J(A, B)$$

The Jaccard distance is metric.

8.4.4 Containment

Definition 8.13 The Containment of set B in A is:

$$C(A, B) = \frac{|A \cap B|}{|A|}$$

Containment is an asymmetric measure and therefore not metric.

8.4.5 Overlap Coefficient

Definition 8.14 The overlap coefficient between sets A and B.

$$overlap(X, Y) = \frac{|A \cap B|}{\min(|X|, |Y|)}$$

The overlap coefficient is not metric.

8.4.6 Tversky Index

Definition 8.15 The Tversky Index of sets X and Y is:

$$S(X, Y) = \frac{|X \cap Y|}{|A \cap B| + \alpha|X - Y| + \beta|Y - X|}$$

The Tversky index is an asymmetric measure and therefore not metric.

8.5 Set of Vectors Similarity

A set of vectors can be compared using the minimum matching distance [5], which constructs a minimum weight matching between pairs of vectors in each set. This distance is metric and can be evaluated in polynomial time.

8.6 Tree Similarity

Trees can be compared for equality using tree isomorphism. Ordered trees are trees such that the children of each node are in a specific sequence. Ordered trees are significantly more efficient to process than unordered trees. Approximate matching and similarity between trees can also be found using the tree edit distance [6]. The tree edit distance is metric. Alternatives to the tree edit distance include using the largest common subtree as an indicator of similarity. These are similar to the graph based version of the problem and are shown in the next section.

Definition 8.16   The tree edit distance between two graphs $d : T_1 \times T_2 \rightarrow \mathbb{N}$ is the minimum number of edge or vertex insertions, deletions, and substitutions to transform one tree to the other.

8.7 Graph Similarity

8.7.1 Graph Isomorphism

Graphs can be tested for structural equality by graph isomorphism testing. Graph isomorphism has not been demonstrated to belong to the complexity class P but it has not been proven to be in NP either.

Definition 8.17   Let $g_1 = (V_1, \alpha_1, \beta_1)$ and $g_2 = (V_2, \alpha_2, \beta_2)$ be two graphs. A graph isomorphism between g_1 and g_2 is a bijective mapping $f : V_1 \rightarrow V_2$ such that

$$\alpha_1(x) = \alpha_2(f(x)) \forall x \in V_1$$
$$\beta_1((x,y)) = \beta_2((f(x),f(y))) \forall (x,y) \in V_1 \times V_1$$

.

If $V_1 = V_2 = 0$ then f is called the empty graph isomorphism

8.7.2 Graph Edit Distance

A harder problem is calculating the approximate similarity or distance between two graphs. The two main approaches are the graph edit distance and using the maximum common subgraph. The graph edit distance is metric. These problems are proven not to belong to P. However, polynomial time approximate solutions exist to the graph edit distance.

Definition 8.18   The graph edit distance $d : G_1 \times G_2 \rightarrow \mathbb{N}$ between two graphs is the minimum sum cost of basic edit operations to transform one graph to another.

8.7.3 Maximum Common Subgraph

Definition 8.19 Let $g_1 = (V_1, \alpha_1, \beta_1)$ and $g_2 = (V_2, \alpha_2, \beta_2)$ be two graphs and $g_1' \subseteq g_1, g_2' \subseteq g_2$. If there exists a graph isomorphism between g_1' and g_2', then both g_1' and g_2' are called a common subgraph of g_1 and g_2.

Definition 8.20 Let g_1 and g_2 be two graphs. A graph g is called the maximum common subgraph of g_1 and g_2 if g is a common subgraph of g_1 and g_2 and there exists no other common subgraph of g_1 and g_2 that has more nodes than g.

Definition 8.21 The distance between graphs g_1 and g_2 is:

$$d(g_1, g_2) = \frac{|MCS(g_1, g_2)|}{|g1|} \text{ where } |g| = |V| + |E|.$$

Definition 8.22 The distance between graphs g_1 and g_2 is:

$$d(g_1, g_2) = \frac{|MCS(g_1, g_2)|}{\max(|g_1|, |g_2|)} \text{ where } |g| = |V| + |E|.$$

An approximate or inexact maximum common subgraph is also possible.

Definition 8.23 The graph edit distance between two graphs $d : G_1 \times G_2 \to \mathbb{N}$ is the minimum number of edge or vertex insertions, deletions, and substitutions to transform one graph to the other.

Distances based on the maximum common subgraph are not metric.

References

1. Peter NY (1993) Data structures and algorithms for nearest neighbor search in general metric spaces. In: Proceedings of the fourth annual ACM-SIAM symposium on discrete algorithms, Austin, Texas, United States. Society for industrial and applied mathematics, pp 311–321
2. Vieira MR, Chino FJT, Traina C Jr., Traina AJM (2004) DBM-Tree: a dynamic metric access method sensitive to local density data. In: Brazilian symposium on databases, Brazil, pp 163–177
3. Paolo C, Marco P, Pavel Z (1997) M-tree: an efficient access method for similarity search in metric spaces. Paper presented at the proceedings of the 23rd international conference on very large data bases
4. Cilibrasi R, Vitányi PMB (2005) Clustering by compression. Inf Theory IEEE Trans 51(4):1523–1545
5. Brecheisen S (2007) Efficient and effective similarity search on complex objects. Ludwig-Maximilians-Universität München, Munich, Germany
6. Bille P (2005) A survey on tree edit distance and related problems. Theor Comput Sci 337(1–3):217–239

Chapter 9
Software Similarity Searching and Classification

Abstract The ultimate problem of this book is to search for similar software to our query from a database and to classify a program as belonging to a particular class. This chapter examines how we transform the pair-wise similarity problem into a similarity search problem over a database. Moreover, we examine statistical classification of birthmarks to identify the class of software it belongs to.

Keywords Software similarity search · Software classification · Similarity search · Instance-based learning · Nearest neighbour · Metric trees · Locality sensitive hashing · Kernel methods

9.1 Instance-Based Learning and Nearest Neighbour

Instance-based learning is a form of machine learning used in classification. To classify an object, it is compared to known instances of that object. If the query is similar to a known instance, or alternatively closest to an instance, known as its nearest neighbour, then it is classified as belonging to the same class. Nearest neighbour and range searches are the fundamental basis for software similarity using software features. If a piece of software represented as an object is in very close range or distance to known software instances, then it is declared a variant (Fig. 9.1).

9.1.1 k Nearest Neighbours Query

Definition 9.1 Given a set of objects P and a query Q, and an integer $k > 0$, the k nearest neighbours (kNN) query is to find a result set kNN that consists of k objects such that for any $p \in (P - kNN)$ and any $p' \in kNN, dist(p', q) \leq dist(p, q)$.

S. Cesare and Y. Xiang, *Software Similarity and Classification*,
SpringerBriefs in Computer Science, DOI: 10.1007/978-1-4471-2909-7_9,
© The Author(s) 2012

Fig. 9.1 The software
similarity search to detect
malware

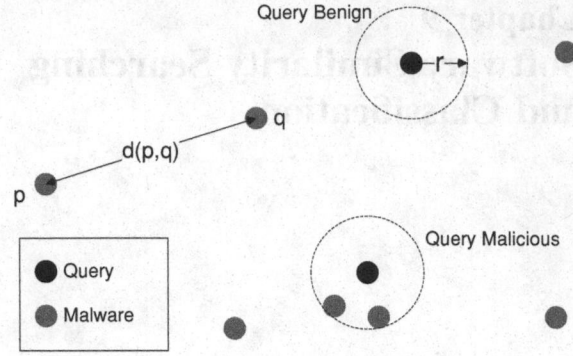

9.1.2 Range Query

Definition 9.2 Given a set of objects P and a query Q, and a range $r > 0$, the range query is to find a result set rNN that consists of objects such that for any $p' \in rNN, dist(p', q) \leq r$.

9.1.3 Metric Trees

Metric trees allow similarity searches (nearest neighbour and range searches) for objects that have a metric distance function. A number of algorithms have been proposed such as BK Trees [1], Vantage Point trees [2], M-Trees [3], Slim trees [4], or DBM Trees [5]. Metric access methods can be categorized by different qualities such as whether the data structures allow for efficient insertion and deletion of objects allowing for dynamic access, or whether the data structures are kept in main memory or on disk.

9.1.4 Locality Sensitive Hashing

Locality sensitive hashing [6] is a scheme whereby similar objects are hashed to the same buckets. This allows a similarity search to perform nearest neighbour searches by hashing.

Definition 9.3 Let d be a metric distance function. Let $B(v, r) = \{q \in X | (v, q) \leq r\}$. A family $H = \{h : S \to U\}$ is called $\{r_1, r_2, p_1, p_2\}$ sensitive for D if for any $v, q \in S$

- If $v \in B(q, r_1)$ then $\Pr_H[h(q) = h(v)] \geq p_1$
- If $v \notin B(q, r_2)$ then $\Pr_H[h(q) = h(v)] \leq p_2$

In order of a locality-sensitive hash (LSH) family to be useful, it has to satisfy inequalities $p_1 > p_2$ and $r_1 < r_2$.

9.1.5 Distributed Similarity Search

Scalability becomes a problem when database sizes increase. For example, malware databases have been growing exponentially [7] and efficient algorithms are required to handle the problem. Distributed algorithms are one solution to scale similarity searches. Distributed metric space similarity search algorithms include M-Chord [8] and GHT* [9, 10]. An approach based on Locality Sensitive Hashing is proposed in [11].

9.2 Statistical Machine Learning

Statistical classification is the process of assigning objects to classes. A typical example is the malware classification problem which is the process of assigning an unknown executable to the class of malicious or non malicious software.

Machine learning can be supervised or unsupervised. In the unsupervised model, none of the objects are labelled, and their class designation is unknown. The usual approach is to perform clustering to identify separate classes. In the supervised approach, a training set of data is labelled and used to build a model of classes in relation to their characteristics. After training, the system classifies unlabelled data and determines their classes.

Statistical classifiers include the popular and efficient Bayesian classifiers. Artificial Neural Networks (ANN) are another popular choice. The classifiers can also be grouped into linear and non linear systems. In a linear classifier, the input space can divide the classes using hyperplanes.

Vectors are used in many machine learning algorithms so often it is most useful to represent software as feature vectors. Features that are extracted from software can be used to construct feature vectors. Kernel machines provide an alternative approach to using feature effects and the most popular kernel method based classifier is the Support Vector Machine [12]. In this approach, a kernel for a particular object must be constructed. For classification of objects such as graphs, a variety of graph kernels can be used.

9.2.1 Vector Space Models

In the vector space model, a feature vector is constructed in $\mathbb{R}^n$ and classes are separated by partitioning over that space. The original feature vectors may have a high dimensionality, but in reality many of these features may be of low importance or redundant. Dimensionality reduction reduces the size of the feature vector (Fig. 9.2).

Fig. 9.2 A linear classifier
separating two classes

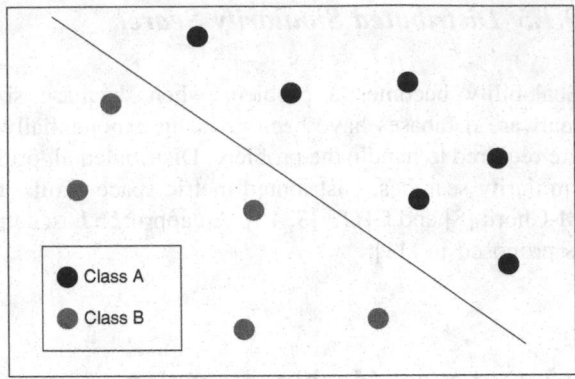

9.2.2 Kernel Methods

The most well known kernel based classifier is the support vector machine (SVM)
[12]. It is a linear classifier and works by constructing a hyperplane that maximally
separates the margins between each class.

9.3 Research Opportunities

Nearest neighbour searches using metric distance functions to perform similarity
searches has been employed in some malware detection literature. Much existing
literature on software similarity has only focused on pairwise similarity and
ignored the indexing and searching problem. Opportunities exist to transfer
existing techniques into metric indexing methods.

Locality sensitive hashing also represents an opportunity as this indexing and
searching technique has not been employed in all areas such as malware detection.
Likewise, distributed similarity search algorithms are still to be exploited in the
domain of software similarity.

The use of kernel methods for graph and tree based features is an area which is
unexplored. The use of graph kernels to enable graph based classification presents
much opportunity for researchers in future work.

References

1. Baeza-Yates R, Navarro G (1998) Fast approximate string matching in a dictionary. In: South
   American symposium on string processing and information retrieval (SPIR'98), pp 14–22
2. Peter NY (1993) Data structures and algorithms for nearest neighbor search in general metric
   spaces. In: Proceedings of the fourth annual ACM-SIAM symposium on discrete algorithms,
   Austin, Texas, United States. Society for Industrial and Applied Mathematics, pp 311–321

3. Paolo C, Marco P, Pavel Z (1997) M-Tree: an efficient access method for similarity search in metric spaces. Paper presented at the proceedings of the 23rd international conference on very large data bases

4. Caetano Traina Jr, Agma JMT, Bernhard S, Christos F (2000) Slim-trees: high performance metric trees minimizing overlap between nodes. Paper presented at the proceedings of the 7th international conference on extending database technology: advances in database technology

5. Vieira MR, Chino FJT, Traina C, Jr, Traina AJM (2004) DBM-Tree: a dynamic metric access method sensitive to local density data. In: Brazilian symposium on databases, Brazil pp 163–177

6. Indyk P, Motwani R (1998) Approximate nearest neighbors: towards removing the curse of dimensionality. In: ACM pp 604–613

7. F-Secure (2007) F-Secure reports amount of malware grew by 100% during 2007

8. Novak D, Zezula P (2006) M-Chord: a scalable distributed similarity search structure. Paper presented at the proceedings of the 1st international conference on scalable information systems, Hong Kong

9. Batko M, Gennaro C, Savino P, Zezula P (2004) Scalable similarity search in metric spaces. In: 213–224

10. Batko M, Gennaro C, Zezula P (2005) A scalable nearest neighbor search in p2p systems. Databases, information systems, and peer-to-peer computing, pp 79–92

11. Haghani P, Michel S, Aberer K (2009) Distributed similarity search in high dimensions using locality sensitive hashing. Paper presented at the proceedings of the 12th international conference on extending database technology: advances in database technology, Saint Petersburg, Russia

12. Cortes C, Vapnik V (1995) Support-vector networks. Mach learn 20(3):273–297

Chapter 10
Applications

Abstract This chapter surveys the application specific literature in software similarity and classification. It examines malware classification, software theft detection, plagiarism detection and code clone detection. We group the literature based on the class of program feature that is used to construct birthmarks. Finally, we critically analyse the approaches used.

Keywords Software similarity · Software classification · Malware classification · Software theft detection · Plagiarism detection · Code clone detection

10.1 Malware Classification

10.1.1 Raw Code

An approach employed by commercial Antivirus avoids static analysis by automatically extracting string signatures [1, 2].The main problem with this approach is that polymorphic malware makes string signatures prone to failure when the byte level content changes due to mutation, recompilation, and source code modification.

Kolmogorov complexity is a theoretical measure of the computational complexity, or minimum string length in a universal description language, required to represent an object or set of data. It is a theoretical measure that is not computable. To estimate the Kolmogorov complexity, an object may be compressed and concatenated with the associated decompression routine, to give the approximate minimum string length to describe the object. The observation, when this theory is related to malware, is that similar malware have similar measures of Kolmogorov complexity. This form of analysis occurs on the malwares raw file or section content.

S. Cesare and Y. Xiang, *Software Similarity and Classification*,
SpringerBriefs in Computer Science, DOI: 10.1007/978-1-4471-2909-7_10,
© The Author(s) 2012

Estimating Kolmogorov complexity was proposed in peHash [3] by identifying the compression ratio of a malicious sample that was subsequently used for clustering malware families. Another measure of similarity related to Kolmogorov complexity is the Normalized Compression Distance (NCD). The NCD was used in [4] to cluster worms into families. This approach, like peHash [3], was not used to classify samples as being benign or malicious, but to cluster malicious samples only.

It was the observation in [5] that malware and benign programs can be classified according to a likeness to a compression model for each of the malicious and benign classes. In this research, it was proposed that two compression models be constructed from a two training sets, one of malicious samples, and one of benign samples. To classify a query sample as being malicious or benign, the number of bits required to encode the query was calculated for each compression model. The query was classified by identifying the class that requires the least data to encode the query.

10.1.2 Instructions

An approach that employs static analysis is code normalization [6, 7]. Code normalization canonizes malware before Antivirus string scanning. In [6], static analysis eliminated superfluous control flow by merging redundant control flow nodes together. Instruction sequences within basic blocks that had no effect were also removed using an SMT decision procedure. The malware normalization approach improves on Antivirus detection but does not always effectively canonize a program to a unique form. This can affect the effectiveness and efficiency of malicious code detection.

A simple approach requiring only disassembly is fingerprinting malware based on opcode distributions [8]. An improved approach was proposed by using n-gram analysis of opcode and byte sequences. N-grams and n-perms can identify similarity between malicious programs and build evolutionary trees [9]. N-gram based feature vectors were used in instance-based learning and statistical classification. Statistical classification allowed for the detection of novel and unknown malware in [10, 11]. These systems improve the effectiveness of static string signatures, but instruction level classification has similar problems when the instruction stream changes to any significant degree.

10.1.3 Basic Blocks

Malware classification using the basic blocks of a program has been investigated in [12]. This approach requires disassembly and ideally a reasonable control flow analysis to identify targets of branchs and calls. The edit distance can be used between basic blocks to identify similarity. Existence of a basic block in a malicious sample can be determined using an inverted index or bloom filters. The main problem with this approach is polymorphic malware that changes the instructions within a basic block.

10.1.4 API Calls

The static ordering of system API calls can be extracted and used for malware classification. Association mining was proposed in [13] proposed to detect unknown malicious programs. Dynamic analysis of API calls or the combination of API calls and data flow can also be used as proposed in [14].

10.1.5 Control Flow and Data Flow

Control flow has been shown to be one of the more invariant features of a polymorphic malware and is resistant to byte and instruction level changes. Combining data flow analysis and control flow analysis was proposed in [15, 16]. Annotated flowgraphs combining data flow were compared to signatures, or automata, that describe the malware.

10.1.6 Data Flow

A data flow analysis was proposed in [17] where value set analysis was used to construct signatures.

10.1.7 Call Graph

Interprocedural control flow using the call graphs of a program have been compared to show similarity to existing malware [18–21]. An approach to transform the interprocedural control flow information into a context free grammar, allowing for homomorphism testing using string equality was also proposed in [22].

10.1.8 Control Flow Graphs

Control flow graphs have also been employed in [22–26] using graph edit distances, maximum common subgraphs and decomposition of graphs into small fixed sized subgraphs or decompiled k-grams.

10.2 Software Theft Detection (Static Approaches)

10.2.1 Instructions

Considering the static instruction sequences in control flow graphs was proposed for Java programs in [27]. This approach proposed using control flow graphs to build static instruction traces. The traces were constructed by imposing a tree structure on the control flow graphs and performing tree traversals to generate an ordering of the instructions. To compare traces a sequence alignment algorithm was used. The similarities between traces in control flow graphs were accumulated to generate a program level similarity score.

K-grams were proposed in [28] to compare two programs. In this work, a k-gram was defined as a unique sequence of k instructions as laid out in the executable. The resulting birthmark is a set of k-grams. To compare two programs, set similarity measures were used which parallel the Jaccard index and the detection of subsets.

The operands of instructions have also been proposed as a useful birthmark in Java programs. Reference [29] proposed four birthmarks, one being the sequence of constant values in field variables. Operand stack patterns were proposed in [30, 31]. Operand stack patterns looked at sequences of bytecode that shared operands through the operand stack.

10.2.2 Control Flow

Control flow has been proposed as a static feature from which birthmarks can be constructed [32, 33]. In the proposed approaches, the edges in the control flow graph were used. The instructions in the basic blocks making up the edge were concatenated with each other to construct a possible execution sequence of code. To compare two of these features, the longest common subsequence (LCS) algorithm was used. To compare two sets of these features, as when all the control flow edges are considered, a maximum weight matching was performed on the set of all pairwise comparisons of those features. This matching sum allows for a calculation of similarity.

10.2.3 API Calls

Static API calls were proposed as birthmarks in [34, 35]. The API calls made in each procedure of a program were grouped together in sets. To compare two sets, the Dice coefficient which measures the similarity between two sets was used. To compare two programs, where each program consists of multiple sets, a maximum weight matching was used on the set of all pairwise comparisons between those sets. This matching allows for calculation of similarity.

10.2.4 Object Dependencies

Object inheritance graphs in Java programs and the objects other objects used was proposed in [29] as a birthmark. This paper proposed a total of four birthmarks that could be used for software theft detection.

10.3 Software Theft Detection (Dynamic Approaches)

10.3.1 Instructions

Dynamic extraction of instruction N-grams was proposed in [36]. This is analogous to k-grams and n-grams in the static approach.

10.3.2 Control Flow

An interesting approach to capture the dynamic nature of control flow was proposed in [37]. The control flow is dynamically traced, and the edges in the associated control flow graph labelled. The execution trace generates a sequence of those labels. The sequence is converted into a context free grammar using the SEQUITUR algorithm which is useful in capturing the repetitive nature of dynamic control flow. The grammar produces a graph and the terminal nodes are removed. This final graph is the birthmark. To compare two birthmarks, a maximum common subgraph is used to identify similarity.

10.3.3 API Calls

Dynamic tracing of API class has had a considerable amount of research [38–42]. The dynamic API trace exhibits properties of the programs semantics and is less prone to the problems of obfuscation that static API call traces have. However, triggering all behaviours can be difficult.

10.3.4 Dependence Graphs

A dynamically generated system call dependence graph approach to building a birthmark was employed in [43]. Nodes in the graph represented system calls and control and data dependencies were represented by edges. The graphs, or birthmarks, were compared to show similarity using subgraph isomorphism testing.

10.4 Plagiarism Detection

Plagiarism detection systems often make the distinction between attribute counting and structure based techniques. Attribute counting is based on software metrics, or the frequencies of particular features occurring. Typical approaches include Halstead metrics and other metrics which take into account attributes including the number of tokens, the number of operators, the number of variables, or the number of source lines [44]. Structure based techniques rely on using program structure which typically include the use of dependency graphs or parse trees.

10.4.1 Raw Code and Tokens

JPlag [45] and YAP3 [46] consider tokens from source code as features and perform similarity comparisons using greedy string tiling. Another approach [47] considers tokenization and linearization of the source code and uses an adaptive sequence alignment to construct a similarity measure.

10.4.2 Parse Trees

Parse trees are related to abstract syntax trees and have been proposed for plagiarism detection [48] by using tree comparisons to identify similarity. Tree similarity can be based on algorithms including tree edit distances or largest common subtrees.

10.4.3 Program Dependency Graph

GPLAG used program dependency graphs of programs [49]. Similarity between program dependency graphs uses similarity metrics such as the graph edit distances.

10.5 Code Clone Detection

10.5.1 Raw Code and Tokens

Clone detection can be performed on the textual stream in a source file once whitespace and comments are removed [50]. The key concept is that a fingerprint of a code fragment is obtained and then the remainder of the source scanned for possible matching duplicates. More recently [51, 52] has used the token approach with good success in large scale evaluations. Large scale copy and paste clones using a data mining approach was investigated in [53, 54].

10.5.2 Abstract Syntax Tree

An alternative approach is to use the abstract syntax tree of the source to generate a fingerprint [55]. Tree matching can subsequently be used to discover software clones. Abstract syntax trees are more impervious to superficial changes to the textual stream and textual organization of the code.

10.5.3 Program Dependency Graph

Other program abstractions can be used to fingerprint code fragments such as the program dependency graph which is a graph combining control and data dependencies [56].

10.6 Critical Analysis

All applications of software similarity and classification share common themes of feature extraction, similarity functions and statistical classification. The literature reviewed in this chapter should be in the context of the theory presented in this book. Initial work on malware detection was based primarily on the raw code contents. As noted in previous chapters, raw code is ineffective when trying to detect malware variants including polymorphic and metamorphic samples. Instruction opcodes and sequences also face similar problems. Control flow has been used successfully in most of the above applications when perform static analyses. The danger of including data flow as a feature is that the birthmarks created become too specific to the instance of code and therefore suffer the same fate as using byte-level content. Therefore, control flow might be the best choice for the time being. Control flow can be obfuscated however, using packing and other techniques so a trend has been to perform dynamic analysis by running the sample program in a virtualized environment. The feature of choice has been the API calls the program makes. Dynamic analysis is not without fault though and that has also been discussed in previous chapters of this book. Of note, there is a distinction in the literature between the software similarity problem and the software classification problem. Some applications such as software theft detection will always be based upon software similarity. However, applications such as malware detection only care for a signature-less binary classification. Nevertheless, software similarity is still useful for identifying families of malware and attributing authorship of those malicious executables.

References

1. Griffin K, Schneider S, Hu X, Chiueh T (2009) Automatic generation of string signatures for malware detection. In: Recent advances in intrusion detection: 12th international symposium, RAID 2009, Saint-Malo. Springer
2. Kephart JO, Arnold WC (1994) Automatic extraction of computer virus signatures. In: 4th virus bulletin international conference, pp 178–184
3. Wicherski G (2009) peHash: a novel approach to fast malware clustering. In: Usenix workshop on large-scale exploits and emergent threats (LEET'09), Boston
4. Wehner S (2007) Analyzing worms and network traffic using compression. J Comput Secur 15(3):303–320
5. Zhou Y, Inge WM (2008) Malware detection using adaptive data compression. In: Proceedings of the 1st ACM workshop on AISec (AISec '08). ACM New York, pp 53–60
6. Christodorescu M, Kinder J, Jha S, Katzenbeisser S, Veith H (2005) Malware normalization. University of Wisconsin, Madison
7. Andrew W, Rachit M, Mohamed RC, Arun L (2006) Normalizing metamorphic malware using term rewriting. Paper presented at the proceedings of the sixth IEEE international workshop on source code analysis and manipulation
8. Bilar D (2007) Opcodes as predictor for malware. Int J Electron Secur Digit Forensics 1(2):156–168
9. Karim ME, Walenstein A, Lakhotia A, Parida L (2005) Malware phylogeny generation using permutations of code. J Comput Virol 1(1):13–23
10. Perdisci R, Lanzi A, Lee W (2008) McBoost: boosting scalability in malware collection and analysis using statistical classification of executables. In: Proceedings of the 2008 annual computer security applications conference. IEEE Computer Society Washington, pp 301–310
11. Kolter JZ, Maloof MA (2004) Learning to detect malicious executables in the wild. In: International conference on knowledge discovery and data mining, pp 470–478
12. Gheorghescu M (2005) An automated virus classification system. In: Virus bulletin conference, pp 294–300

13. Ye Y, Wang D, Li T, Ye D (2007) IMDS: intelligent malware detection system. In: Proceedings of the 13th ACM SIGKDD international conference on knowledge discovery and data mining. ACM
14. Kolbitsch C, Comparetti PM, Kruegel C, Kirda E, Zhou X, Wang XF, Santa Barbara UC (2009) Effective and efficient malware detection at the end host. In: 18th USENIX security symposium
15. Christodorescu M, Jha S, Seshia SA, Song D, Bryant RE (2005) Semantics-aware malware detection. In: Proceedings of the 2005 IEEE symposium on security and privacy (S&P 2005), Oakland
16. Christodorescu M, Jha S (2003) Static analysis of executables to detect malicious patterns. Paper presented at the proceedings of the 12th USENIX security symposium
17. Leder F, Steinbock B, Martini P (2009) Classification and detection of metamorphic malware using value set analysis. In: Proceedings of 4th international conference on malicious and unwanted software (Malware 2009), Montreal
18. Carrera E, Erdélyi G (2004) Digital genome mapping–advanced binary malware analysis. In: Virus bulletin conference, pp 187–197
19. Briones I, Gomez A (2008) Graphs, entropy and grid computing: automatic comparison of malware. In: Virus bulletin conference, pp 1–12
20. Hu X, Chiueh T, Shin KG (2009) Large-scale malware indexing using function-call graphs. In: computer and communications security, Chicago. ACM, pp 611–620
21. Dullien T, Rolles R (2005) Graph-based comparison of executable objects (English version). In: SSTIC
24. Cesare S, Xiang Y (2011) Malware variant detection using similarity search over sets of control flow graphs. In: IEEE Trustcom
22. Cesare S, Xiang Y (2010) A fast flowgraph based classification system for packed and polymorphic malware on the endhost. In: IEEE 24th international conference on advanced information networking and application (AINA 2010)
23. Kruegel C, Kirda E, Mutz D, Robertson W, Vigna G (2006) Polymorphic worm detection using structural information of executables. Lect Notes Comput Sci 3858:207
25. Cesare S, Xiang Y (2010) Classification of malware using structured control flow. In: 8th Australasian symposium on parallel and distributed computing (AusPDC 2010)
26. Bonfante G, Kaczmarek M, Marion JY (2008) Morphological detection of malware. In: International conference on malicious and unwanted software, IEEE, Alexendria 1–8 Oct 2008
27. Park H, Choi S, Lim H, Han T (2008) Detecting code theft via a static instruction trace birthmark for Java methods. In IEEE, pp 551–556
28. Myles G, Collberg C (2005) K-gram based software birthmarks. Paper presented at the proceedings of the 2005 ACM symposium on applied computing, Santa Fe
29. Tamada H, Nakamura M, Monden A, Matsumoto KI (2005) Java birthmarks-detecting the software theft. IEICE Trans Inf Syst E Ser D 88(9):2148
30. Lim H, Park H, Choi S, Han T (2008) Detecting theft of java applications via a static birthmark based on weighted stack patterns. IEICE Trans Inf Syst E91-D(9):2323–2332
31. Park H, Lim H, Choi S, Han T (2008) A static java birthmark based on operand stack behaviors. In: Proceedings of the 2008 international conference on information security and assurance (ISA 2008), pp 133–136
32. Lim H, Park H, Choi S, Han T (2009) A static java birthmark based on control flow edges. In: Computer software and applications conference (COMPSAC '09). IEEE, pp 413–420
33. Lim H, Park H, Choi S, Han T (2009) A method for detecting the theft of Java programs through analysis of the control flow information. Inf Softw Technol 51(9):1338–1350
34. Choi S, Park H, Lim H, Han T (2009) A static API birthmark for Windows binary executables. J Syst Softw 82(5):862–873
35. Choi S, Park H, Lim H, Han T (2008) A static birthmark of binary executables based on API call structure. Advances in computer science—ASIAN 2007 computer and network security, pp 2–16

36. Lu B, Liu F, Ge X, Liu B, Luo X (2007) A software birthmark based on dynamic opcode n-gram. In: Proceedings of the international conference on semantic computing (ICSC '07). IEEE computer society
37. Myles G, Collberg C (2004) Detecting software theft via whole program path birthmarks. Information security, pp 404–415
38. Moriyama O, Furue T, Tooyama T, Matsumoto T (2006) A method of software dynamic birthmarks using history of API function calls. In: IEIC technical report (Institute of Electronics, Information and Communication Engineers), vol 106(235), pp 77–84
39. Schuler D, Dallmeier V, Lindig C (2007) A dynamic birthmark for java. Paper presented at the proceedings of the twenty-second IEEE/ACM international conference on automated software engineering, Atlanta
40. Tamada H, Okamoto K, Nakamura M, Monden A, Matsumoto K (2004) Dynamic software birthmarks to detect the theft of windows applications. In: International symposium on future software technology (ISFST 2004)
41. Tamada H, Okamoto K, Nakamura M, Monden A, Ichi Matsumoto K (2007) Design and evaluation of dynamic software birthmarks based on API calls. Nara Institute of Science and Technology, Technical Report
42. Schuler D, Dallmeier V (2006) Detecting software theft with API call sequence sets. In: Proceedings of the 8th workshop software reengineering, Bad Honnef
43. Wang X, Jhi Y-C, Zhu S, Liu P (2009) Behavior based software theft detection. Paper presented at the proceedings of the 16th ACM conference on computer and communications security, Chicago
44. Jones EL (2001) Metrics based plagarism monitoring. J Comput Sci Coll 16(4):253–261
45. Prechelt L, Malpohl G, Philippsen M (2002) Finding plagiarisms among a set of programs with JP lag. J Univers Comput Sci 8(11):1016–1038
46. Wise MJ (1996) YAP3: improved detection of similarities in computer program and other texts. SIGCSE Bull 28(1):130–134. doi:10.1145/236462.236525
47. Ji J-H, Woo G, Cho H-G (2007) A source code linearization technique for detecting plagiarized programs. SIGCSE Bull 39(3):73–77. doi:10.1145/1269900.1268807
48. Son J-W, Park S-B, Park S-Y (2006) Program plagiarism detection using parse tree kernels. In: Yang Q, Webb G (eds) PRICAI 2006: Trends in artificial intelligence, vol 4099. Lecture notes in computer science. Springer Berlin/Heidelberg, pp 1000–1004. doi:10.1007/978-3-540-36668-3_122
49. Liu C, Chen C, Han J, Yu PS (2006) GPLAG: detection of software plagiarism by program dependence graph analysis. Paper presented at the proceedings of the 12th ACM SIGKDD international conference on knowledge discovery and data mining, Philadelphia
50. Ducasse S, Rieger M, Demeyer S (1999) A language independent approach for detecting duplicated code. Published by the IEEE Computer Society, p 109
51. Kamiya T, Kusumoto S, Inoue K (2002) CCFinder: a multilinguistic token-based code clone detection system for large scale source code. IEEE Trans Softw Eng, pp 654–670
52. Livieri S, Higo Y, Matushita M, Inoue K (2007) Very-large scale code clone analysis and visualization of open source programs using distributed CCFinder: D-CCFinder. In: Proceedings of the 29th international conference on software engineering (ICSE '07). IEEE computer society, pp 106–115
53. Li Z, Lu S, Myagmar S, Zhou Y (2004) CP-Miner: a tool for finding copy-paste and related bugs in operating system code. In: Proceedings of the 6th conference on symposium on operating systems design & implementation (OSDI '04). USENIX association, pp 20–20
54. Li Z, Lu S, Myagmar S, Zhou Y (2006) CP-Miner: finding copy-paste and related bugs in large-scale software code. IEEE Trans Softw Eng, pp 176–192
55. Baxter ID, Yahin A, Moura L, Sant'Anna M, Bier L (1998) Clone detection using abstract syntax trees. Published by the IEEE computer society, p 368
56. Krinke J (2001) Identifying similar code with program dependence graphs. Published by the IEEE computer society, p 301

Chapter 11
Future Trends and Conclusion

Abstract This chapter looks at future trends in software similarity and classification research and engineering. We look at the technology becoming unified and its applications in cloud services and mobile platforms. Finally, we conclude the book with some final thoughts.

Keywords Cloud services · Mobile computing · Antivirus

11.1 Future Trends

Software similarity and classification may see the unification of malware classification with other technologies such as software theft detection or software clone detection. These topics will see sharing of concepts and techniques and the use of program features will become comprehensive. It may indicate that a combination approach to software similarity and classification is appropriate. Many of the features are useful at representing a particular property of software, but obfuscations or transformations may alter these properties. Using a variety of properties in combination may be a suitable response for increasing accuracy.

Static binary analysis is an emerging field and continues to improve. The analyses are becoming stronger and able to model more complex behaviour without gross under-approximations or over-approximations. This will continue to improve as this area of static analysis becomes more recognized. In particular, malware classification and software theft detection are driving forces of the need for analyses.

Static binary analysis is used in academic malware classification. It has not seen widespread use in commercial Antivirus. We believe this situation will change due to the more effective signatures and the ability to use machine learning and statistical classification to detect novel samples of malware. The trend in malware classification is to use higher level of abstractions and more emphasis is placed on combining data flow analysis with control flow analysis. Appropriate database technologies are being used more as the problem is becoming how to effectively perform indexing and searching of program features for an instance-based signature approach of malware variant detection. Statistical classification continues to improve on the effectiveness of program features used. We are likely to see the combination of program features, and the combination of different classifiers to improve system accuracy. Complex objects such as graphs will continue to be used with an emphasis on problems in graph mining.

Software theft detection is not widely used by all vendors, but as technology improves and matures, this may become more common. Software theft detection is a program variant detection problem and therefore uses instance-based learning. Database technology as in the case of malware variant detection will take important roles.

Network speeds are improving and cloud services are becoming more popular. Antivirus vendors have already taken advantage of this and have provided an initial set of offerings for cloud based malware detection. Services already exist that provide AV scanning on demand using a large number of commercial scanners. A hybrid scheme may also be used where some of the processing and feature extraction is done on the endpoint. We expect that as bandwidth becomes less of an issue, cloud Antivirus will become popular. Placing malware classification in the cloud allows the use of huge signature databases along with correlation not possible when end users are disconnected. Mobile platforms are less powerful than their desktop counterparts, so these devices would benefit from cloud services where the majority of processing is done away from the user's device. Finally, cloud services may provide an opportunity to detect attackers, through service misuse, from tuning their malware or plagiarised code to evade detection.

11.2 Conclusion

In conclusion, software similarity and classification is an important topic that unifies and tackles the problems of malware classification, plagiarism detection, software theft detection and code clone detection. Many techniques are pioneered or formalized in one topic but only later applied, if at all, to other domains. We have presented the core concepts of how to approach this problem and identify new areas of research. Much research is possible simply by applying existing research across domains.